Vol. CIX   No. 2

D1267877

Aduit
Bible Class

SPRING QUARTER   March, April, May 2023

Editor in Chief: Kenneth Sponsler

Union
Gospel
Press

Edited and published quarterly by
THE INCORPORATED TRUSTEES OF THE
GOSPEL WORKER SOCIETY
UNION GOSPEL PRESS DIVISION
Rev. W. B. Musselman, Founder

Price: $4.39 per quarter*
shipping and handling extra

ISBN 978-1-64495-285-6

Pleasing the Father Through Jesus

BY KENNETH SPONSLER

Our lessons this quarter focus on a grand theme: how Jesus lived a life that was completely pleasing to God the Father. Jesus pleased the Father in everything—in His works, in giving Himself as the Sacrifice for our sins, and in His teachings. No one else on earth before or since has ever managed to do this.

Yet because Jesus thoroughly pleased the Father, there is hope for us. Through His sacrifice, we are washed clean of our sin, and through the indwelling of His Spirit we are enabled to live a life of righteousness that will be pleasing to our Heavenly Father. We will not do so perfectly or without stumbling in this life, but God has set us on a path to glory on which He will unfailingly lead us.

And we have yet another amazing provision to help us in our pursuit of pleasing the Father: Jesus' perfect example, which we are called to follow (cf. I Pet. 2:21). That is indeed one of the main purposes for our lessons this quarter—that as we examine all the ways in which Jesus pleased His Father, we will be challenged to follow Him in doing so ourselves.

Our first lesson takes us to Jesus' baptism in the Jordan River. It was there that the Father unambiguously announced His full approval of all that Jesus said, did, and thought: "Thou art my beloved Son, in whom I am well pleased" (Mark 1:11). Jesus did not need John's baptism of repentance, but He underwent the observance to identify Himself with all of us, who do need to repent. That already is an example for us.

Lesson 2 takes us to one of the most specific examples for us to follow: how to deal with the enemy's temptations.

Satan came to Jesus when He was weak from physical deprivation and did his utmost to derail Him from His mission. Had Jesus yielded even once, it would have been all over for us—we would be left in darkness and sin. But Jesus' use of the Word of God to meet the devil's enticements provides us the example we need for doing the same.

Our third lesson has much that seems beyond our reach. Indeed, we cannot raise anyone from the dead, as Jesus proclaims the Son was given authority to do, or act as Judge of all people. But Jesus' main point, that He always followed His Father's example (John 5:19), should also be true of us. In all things we should strive to do what we see Jesus doing—showing the love of the Father to people and proclaiming His truth.

When it comes to Jesus' sacrifice, we cannot bear anyone else's sins (we cannot even bear our own!), but we are each called to take up our own cross in following Him. If we find the prospect of sacrifice hard to bear, we should look to Jesus' example in the Garden (lesson 4). He found the prospect dreadful to the extreme, yet He accepted the Father's will and entrusted Himself to Him. We can and must do likewise.

In bearing the punishment for our sins, Jesus did the ultimate in pleasing His Father (lesson 5). We can please the Father by accepting what He did for us and following in His steps in accepting our share of suffering for God's glory, as I Peter 2:21, noted earlier, makes clear.

Lesson 6 brings us to Easter and Jesus' triumphant resurrection. The resurrection was the Father's ultimate stamp of approval on Jesus' life and sacrifice (cf. Rom. 1:4). What is equally amazing is that in His grace the Father has raised us with Him in newness of life (6:4-5).

Once Jesus had risen from death, He could have ascended to the Father immediately. But He stayed behind long enough to encourage His disciples and open their minds to the truths written about Him (lesson 7). They needed this instruction, for they would soon be proclaiming these truths to all people. His mission was now theirs, and today it has been passed on to us.

With lesson 8 we turn to specific portions of Jesus' teachings. He pleased His Father by teaching God's truth, and we can please Him as well by faithfully teaching the same truths, recorded in His Word. The truths we will look at concern who Jesus is and what He has done for us.

Lesson 8 focuses on the profound truth that we find true life only in Jesus, for He is the Bread of Life. This was a difficult teaching for those who first heard it, but God is pleased when we seek understanding from Him and accept it unreservedly by faith.

In lesson 9 we see Jesus presented as the Light of the World. Only by following Him can we be delivered from walking in darkness. When we trust Him, we are trusting the One who sent Him, and we walk in His light.

In lesson 10 Jesus assures us that He is our Good Shepherd, who gives His life for the sheep (us). He makes the specific point that the Father loves Him "because I lay down my life, that I might take it again" (John 10:17). We can rejoice that He gave His life for us but took it again to remain our living Shepherd.

That Jesus has conquered death for us becomes fully explicit in lesson 11, where He declares Himself to be the

Resurrection and the Life. Again, we have His assurance, "Whosoever liveth, and believeth in me shall never die" (John 11:26).

Lesson 12 is our last on Jesus' teachings about Himself. Here He draws His famous analogy of the vine. He is the Vine; we are the branches. The branches are kept alive only as they remain in the Vine; so we must remain in Him. As we do, we are assured of much fruitfulness and that we will bring glory to God.

Our final lesson shifts gears somewhat. Instead of hearing a proclamation about Himself, we are allowed into the hallowed chamber of Jesus' prayer to the Father on our behalf. There we learn how much we are on His heart and how much He wants us to be one with Him and the Father. May we have joyful confidence in His powerful intercession!

SCRIPTURE LESSON TEXT

MARK 1:4 John did baptize in the wilderness, and preach the baptism of repentance for the remission of sins.

5 And there went out unto him all the land of Judaea, and they of Jerusalem, and were all baptized of him in the river of Jordan, confessing their sins.

6 And John was clothed with camel's hair, and with a girdle of a skin about his loins; and he did eat locusts and wild honey;

7 And preached, saying, There cometh one mightier than I after me, the latchet of whose shoes I am not worthy to stoop down and unloose.

8 I indeed have baptized you with water: but he shall baptize you with the Holy Ghost.

9 And it came to pass in those days, that Jesus came from Nazareth of Galilee, and was baptized of John in Jordan.

10 And straightway coming up out of the water, he saw the heavens opened, and the Spirit like a dove descending upon him:

11 And there came a voice from heaven, *saying,* Thou art my beloved Son, in whom I am well pleased.

12 And immediately the Spirit driveth him into the wilderness.

13 And he was there in the wilderness forty days, tempted of Satan; and was with the wild beasts; and the angels ministered unto him.

NOTES

4

Jesus' Baptism

Lesson Text: Mark 1:4-13

Related Scriptures: Matthew 3:1-17; Luke 3:15-22;
Matthew 17:1-7; Mark 9:2-8; Luke 9:28-36

TIME: A.D. 26   PLACES: wilderness of Judea; Jordan River

GOLDEN TEXT—"There came a voice from heaven, saying, Thou art my beloved Son, in whom I am well pleased" (Mark 1:11).

Lesson Exposition

THE PREPARER—Mark 1:4-8

John's ministry (Mark 1:4-5). The three Synoptic Gospel authors (Matthew, Mark, and Luke) all introduce the forerunner of Christ, that is, John the Baptizer, before describing the beginning of Christ's ministry. John was the son of the priest Zacharias (Luke 1:5-25, 57-63), so he could have been involved in a ministry in the temple in Jerusalem. Instead of ministering in such dignified surroundings, however, he did his work in the wilderness. Since his ministry centered around baptizing people, he is called John the Baptist in all three Synoptic Gospels (Matt. 3:1; Mark 6:14; Luke 7:28).

John ministered as a herald, or announcer, for the arrival of the Messiah. Important Roman officials were always preceded by a herald, so when one arrived in town, everyone knew someone significant was coming.

John's "baptism of repentance" (Mark 1:4) should not be confused with Christian baptism. Today, following their conversion, believers are baptized in a ceremony that pictures the death, burial, and resurrection of Christ, all of which are past. John's baptism was preparatory for the coming of the Messiah. Baptism was known to the Jews, for it was required of Gentiles entering into Judaism. John's baptism, however, was for the Jews, God's covenant people, and it required repentance in anticipation of the arrival of the Messiah.

Those who were baptized by John gave testimony to the fact that they had repented of their sins and as a result were forgiven. Forgiveness was not a result of the baptism but of their repentance.

The concept of repentance is important for us. It means "to think differently" or "to reverse a pattern of thought." Implied in the term is the concept that a deliberate change of thought has occurred and led to a change of direction in one's life. A person who has truly repented of sin will experience a changed life.

John's lifestyle (Mark 1:6). John appeared on the stage of history as the last of the Old Testament line of prophets. According to Jesus' statements in Luke 7:24-28, he was the fulfillment of Malachi 3:1. Matthew quoted a longer statement in which Jesus indicated that

John was actually the fulfillment of the Elijah prophecy in Malachi 4:5, but it required faith to accept this (Matt. 11:14). When the angel appeared to Zacharias announcing John's birth, he said John would minister in the spirit and power of Elijah (Luke 1:17). All these statements pointed to John's ministry as the forerunner of the Messiah.

John's attire would have reminded the Jewish people of Elijah, the premier Old Testament prophet. His attire and diet were characteristic of someone who spent his time residing in a wilderness area. They marked him out as very different. It was his choice to live frugally and apply himself wholeheartedly to the ministry God had given him.

John's message (Mark 1:7-8). In Mark's text John revealed his genuinely humble attitude in the statement "There cometh one mightier than I after me, the latchet of whose shoes I am not worthy to stoop down and unloose." The task of removing the sandals of a guest was relegated to the lowest servant in a household.

This One would baptize them with the Holy Spirit instead of water. In the course of Israel's history, several identifying signs had been given to them. In Abraham's day the sign of circumcision was given to indicate the covenant relationship God had established with His chosen ones. In Moses' day the sign of Sabbath observance was given in the law, indicating that God had a special relationship with this nation He had just brought out of Egypt. In John's day the sign of a right relationship with God was water baptism.

When the Messiah Himself arrived, however, the sign was going to be baptism with the Holy Spirit. He would be given as a gift to all who became God's children through salvation. "The One who would give the Spirit as an identifying sign of relationship would be the true Messiah—not the one who gave the external preparatory sign. Messiah's baptism would not be external but internal" (Pentecost, *The Words and Works of Jesus Christ,* Zondervan).

THE PREPARED—Mark 1:9-13

Jesus' baptism (Mark 1:9). Jesus was now "about thirty years of age" (Luke 3:23). Although His baptism was immediately followed by Satan's temptation in the wilderness, this was the beginning of His public ministry. Matthew gives us a bit of information not found in either Mark or Luke, namely, that John initially objected to baptizing Jesus: "But John forbad him, saying, I have need to be baptized of thee, and comest thou to me?" (3:14). Jesus insisted, telling him it was "to fulfil all righteousness" (vs. 15).

Since John's baptism was done as an external evidence of a person's repentance of sin, and since Jesus had never sinned, there was no need for Jesus to be baptized in the same way as other people. His baptism, therefore, had to fulfill other purposes rather than giving evidence of repentance. It was also not the same as today's Christian baptism, for there was not yet a death, burial, and resurrection with which to be identified. Jesus' baptism, therefore, was different from all others.

The summary given in *The Bible Knowledge* Commentary (Walvoord and Zuck, eds., Victor) offers reasons for Jesus' baptism:

"Mark did not state why Jesus submitted to John's baptism; however, three reasons may be suggested: (1) It was an act of obedience, showing that Jesus was in full agreement with God's overall plan and the role of John's baptism in it (cf. Matt. 3:15). (2) It was an act of self-identification with the nation of Israel whose heritage and sinful predicament He shared (cf. Isa. 53:12). (3) It was an act of self-dedication to His messianic mission, signifying His official acceptance and entrance into it."

Jesus' approval (Mark 1:10-11). The word "straightway" means "directly" or "at once" and could be translated "immediately." This word occurs forty-two times in Mark, furthering the concept of Jesus as a Servant eager to do His Father's will. John baptized Jesus in the Jordan River, and as they were coming up out of the water, there was an immediate display of God's approval of His Son. The heavens opened and the Holy Spirit descended upon Jesus while the voice of God the Father lovingly addressed His Son, who pleased Him greatly.

It is important to realize that the description given here is not of an actual dove but rather of the descent of the Spirit in a form similar to that of a dove. Luke 3:22 says the "Holy Ghost descended in a bodily shape like a dove upon him." There was a definite form visible, but the word "like" indicates only a similarity, not the exact same thing.

The voice from heaven expressed God's approval of Jesus and the ministry on which He was embarking.

Jesus' temptation (Mark 1:12-13). While all three Synoptic Gospels say that Jesus went into the wilderness to be tempted after His baptism, only Mark indicates that it was immediate and forceful. The word "driveth" indicates He was thrust under a strong, constraining impulse from the Spirit. This is much more forceful than Matthew and Luke, which describe Him as being led or brought by the Spirit (Matt. 4:1; Luke 4:1). What is significant about this is the fact that He was not driven there by Satan but rather by the Holy Spirit of God.

The impression this gives us is that Jesus took the offensive in the battle with temptation and evil. This was a case of God the Father putting His Son to the test and proving Him to be free of sin and eminently qualified to fulfill His messianic role. Of course, it was also a case of Satan doing his best to entice Him away from that role in order to ruin the plan of redemption.

The fact that Jesus could truly be tempted proves His humanity. He was not exempt from Satan's attacks and can therefore fully identify with us when we face them. Hebrews 2:18 assures us, "For in that he himself hath suffered being tempted, he is able to succour (help) them that are tempted." While it is impossible for us as sinners to live according to all the demands of the law, Jesus fulfilled that law by coming in the flesh and being victorious over temptation.

—*Keith E. Eggert.*

QUESTIONS

1. What was John's primary ministry, and what activity was that ministry centered around?
2. What were people indicating when they were baptized by John?
3. What is repentance, and what results when a person repents?
4. Why was the comparison of John with Elijah important?
5. How did John convey his recognition of the Messiah's greatness?
6. What made Jesus' baptism different from all other baptisms?
7. What does the term "straightway" indicate in the Gospel of Mark?
8. What occurred that confirmed to Jesus that He was pleasing God?
9. Why is it important to note that Jesus was led, or driven, by the Spirit into the wilderness to be tempted?
10. Why are the results of Jesus' temptation important to us?

—*Keith E. Eggert.*

PRACTICAL POINTS

1. Religious rites mean nothing apart from the confession of sins that brings divine forgiveness (Mark 1:4-5).
2. God's work demands faithfulness, not conformity to society's standards (vs. 6).
3. There is no place for self-promotion in serving the Lord; He must be preeminent (vss. 7-8).
4. The presence and power of the Lord are essential to serving Him successfully (vss. 9-11).
5. The Holy Spirit never leads us into difficult places and then abandons us (vs. 12).
6. With God's help we can endure any temptation (vs. 13).

—Jarl K. Waggoner.

RESEARCH AND DISCUSSION

1. In what ways did John the Baptist's ministry differ from Jesus' (Mark 1:4- 5, 8; cf. Matt. 3:1-12; 4:17)?
2. How might John's unusual appearance have helped or hindered his ministry (Mark 1:6)? Why are we so quick to judge others on the basis of appearance?
3. How would you characterize the ministry of John the Baptist? Why was it so important?
4. What similarities are there between Jesus' baptism and the believer's water baptism (Mark 1:10-11)? How are they different (cf. Matt. 28:19)?
5. Why is it important to us in a practical sense that Jesus was "tempted of Satan" (Mark 1:13)?

—Jarl K. Waggoner.

Golden Text Illuminated

"There came a voice from heaven, saying, Thou art my beloved Son, in whom I am well pleased" (Mark 1:11).

The baptism of Jesus was a turning point in His life. Behind Him were thirty years of formative growth, the adult portion of which was spent as a tradesman in Nazareth. The arrival of John the Baptist on the scene signaled that it was time for Jesus to lay aside His trade and begin His ministry, which was the reason for His coming.

Jesus' baptism by John demonstrated His identification with sinners, though He Himself was sinless. It was the righteous thing to do, for it was God's will for Him (Matt. 3:15); likewise, baptism is God's will for all believers. It is our way of publicly identifying with the death, burial, and resurrection of our Lord.

Jesus' baptism also was the opportune time for the Father to send the Spirit to Him to empower Him as needed in the days ahead. The first ministry of the Spirit in Jesus' life was to send Him to the desert to be tested and then to enable Him in various ways and at numerous times for the rest of His earthly ministry (Luke 4:14).

Jesus was prepared for leadership by the Spirit's enabling, and by His obedient life He pleased His heavenly Father immensely. So much was the Father pleased at the baptism of our Lord that He spoke in an audible voice from heaven to announce that fact.

God is pleased with us when we have chosen to identify with His Son by baptism. We should accept His pleasure by faith, however, rather than look for some sign from heaven.

—Darrell W. McKay.

Scripture Lesson Text

MATT. 4:1 Then was Jesus led up of the Spirit into the wilderness to be tempted of the devil.

2 And when he had fasted forty days and forty nights, he was afterward an hungred.

3 And when the tempter came to him, he said, If thou be the Son of God, command that these stones be made bread.

4 But he answered and said, It is written, Man shall not live by bread alone, but by every word that proceedeth out of the mouth of God.

5 Then the devil taketh him up into the holy city, and setteth him on a pinnacle of the temple,

6 And saith unto him, If thou be the Son of God, cast thyself down: for it is written, He shall give his angels charge concerning thee: and in *their* **hands they shall bear thee up, lest at any time thou dash thy foot against a stone.**

7 Jesus said unto him, It is written again, Thou shalt not tempt the Lord thy God.

8 Again, the devil taketh him up into an exceeding high mountain, and sheweth him all the kingdoms of the world, and the glory of them;

9 And saith unto him, All these things will I give thee, if thou wilt fall down and worship me.

10 Then saith Jesus unto him, Get thee hence, Satan: for it is written, Thou shalt worship the Lord thy God, and him only shalt thou serve.

11 Then the devil leaveth him, and, behold, angels came and ministered unto him.

12 Now when Jesus had heard that John was cast into prison, he departed into Galilee;

13 And leaving Nazareth, he came and dwelt in Capernaum, which is upon the sea coast, in the borders of Zabulon and Nephthalim:

14 That it might be fulfilled which was spoken by Esaias the prophet.

NOTES

Overcoming Temptation with the Word

Lesson Text: Matthew 4:1-14a

Related Scriptures: Luke 4:1-13; I Corinthians 10:9-13; I John 2:12-14

TIME: A.D. 26   PLACE: wilderness of Judea

GOLDEN TEXT—"But he answered and said, It is written, Man shall not live by bread alone, but by every word that proceedeth out of the mouth of God" (Matthew 4:4).

Lesson Exposition

PREPARATION FOR TEMPTATION—Matt. 4:1-2

Alone in the wilderness (Matt. 4:1). In Matthew's record of the life of Jesus, the high point of Jesus' baptism was followed by a time of severe testing by the devil.

Even though the devil was the agent of the temptation of Jesus, he was not the one who controlled the situation; rather, Jesus was led by the Spirit of God to the place of testing. This is an important fact to note, for it explains how temptation fits into God's plan.

According to James 1:13, God does not tempt any person to sin. Instead, He uses even the malicious motives of the devil to further His own good purposes. What the devil does to destroy Christians God can turn around to develop them in their spiritual strength.

The temptation of Jesus occurred in the wilderness. This barren, desolate land was significant in at least two ways. First, it was a place in which there was little comfort or companionship. Jesus had to endure the devil's attack without physical support or the help of other people. Second, it paralleled the experience of the nation of Israel, who had been tested in the wilderness.

Hungry after fasting (Matt. 4:2). The devil waited as Jesus fasted for forty days until He was very hungry. This, however, was God's will for Him, because the Spirit of God had led Him there. Hunger is a basic and powerful physical drive. Jesus had to decide whether to remain hungry in obedience to God's direction or to seek to satisfy His hunger by disobeying God's direction. The devil would seek to exploit Jesus' extreme hunger in his attempt to undermine His obedience to the Father.

PROCESS OF TEMPTATION— Matt. 4:3-10

Independent use of power (Matt. 4:3-4). The devil is masterful in preparing temptations that appear innocent on the surface but have disastrous consequences. At His baptism, Jesus heard God the Father call Him His beloved Son. The devil picked up that title as he spoke to Jesus. In essence he said, "If You really are the Son of God, use Your power to satisfy Your hunger."

The devil did not doubt that Jesus is the Son of God. Instead, he tried to use Jesus' hunger to drive a wedge between the Son and the Father. All around Jesus were stones, perhaps resembling loaves of bread in their shape and size. The Son of God could easily transform them into bread merely by speaking a word.

Jesus was hungering in the desert because the Spirit of God had directed Him to fast. To use His divine power to satisfy His hunger at this time would have been something of a spiritual declaration of independence. Jesus would not be living under the authority of the Father but following His own way.

Jesus responded to the devil's suggestion by quoting the Word of God. He cited Deuteronomy 8:3, which told of Israel's experience in the wilderness many centuries before. In that passage, God said that He had led Israel into the wilderness in order to determine whether they would keep His commandments (vs. 2). God wanted Israel to know that obedience to His word is the most important value in life, even more important than satisfying physical hunger.

Applying this biblical truth to His own experience, Jesus chose to obey God rather than use His divine power to satisfy His hunger. He passed the first test by keeping obedience to God as the first priority in His life. Jesus did not let physical need blind Him to spiritual values.

Impressive display of power (Matt. 4:5-7). The first test was in the privacy of the wilderness, but the second test occurred in the public setting of Jerusalem. The devil led Jesus to the roof of the temple. The point on the southeast corner of the temple area was some 450 feet above the valley below.

At that highly visible place, the devil challenged Jesus to prove that He really was the Son of God by jumping off. To make the temptation particularly powerful, Satan used Scripture to make his point. Quoting from Psalm 91:11-12, he said that God had promised to send His angels to bear Jesus up.

The devil cleverly misapplied God's Word as he sought to tempt Jesus to sin. The passage in Psalm 91 was never intended to encourage God's people to be careless or to presume upon God's gracious protection. Instead, it promised that God would deliver His people who fell into difficulties as they followed His will.

Once again Jesus countered Satan's temptation by an appeal to Scripture. Satan had taken Psalm 91:11-12 out of context. Jesus, however, used Deuteronomy 6:16 in a way that agreed with its original context. In the Deuteronomy passage, God said, "Ye shall not tempt the Lord your God, as ye tempted him" in the wilderness.

Illegitimate offer of power (Matt. 4:8-10). The first two tests were subtle attempts to get Jesus to work outside the plan of God. The final test was a much more blatant temptation. The devil took Jesus into a very high mountain. Jesus there could see all the kingdoms of the earth before Him.

Jesus knew that the earth rightfully belonged to Him and that He would eventually reign as King over it all.

Before Jesus could wear the crown, however, He had to endure the cross. As Jesus' prayer in the Garden of Gethsemane showed, this was a painful experience for Him to bear. Because of His love, Jesus was willing to die on the cross, but He asked the father if there were some other means that could accomplish the same effect.

Satan made Jesus a tempting offer. He said that he would give all of the earth to Jesus if only He would fall down and worship him. In other words, Satan was saying that Jesus could be King without having to go to the cross.

Jesus rejected this temptation outright. He ordered Satan to leave. Once again He quoted the Bible, which commands that only the Lord is to be worshiped and served (cf. Deut. 6:13). Instead of thinking that the end would justify the means, as we frequently are tempted to suppose, Jesus fixed His focus on worshipping the Lord and obeying His Word.

PROCEEDING AFTER TEMPTATION—Matt. 4:11-14a

Served by angels (Matt. 4:11). Jesus had stood in obedience to the Word and will of God. Although He would face temptations again in His life, for the present the devil left Him. To help Jesus in His weakened, famished condition, angels came and ministered to Him.

Secluded in Galilee (Matt. 4:12). The ministry of John the Baptist was centered in Judea. That part of the country was the heart of Jewish life, so it was where people would expect prophets to minister. Jesus, however, did not fit the typical pattern. His ministry was to have a different geographical focus.

As Matthew 14:3-5 relates, John's forthright preaching brought upon him the wrath of Herod, the Roman-endorsed ruler of the provinces of Galilee and Perea. Herod arrested him and wanted to put him to death.

With John unable to continue his public ministry, it seems the Jewish religious leaders headquartered in Jerusalem turned their attention to Jesus (cf. John 4:1-3). Sensing it was not the time to engage this opposition, Jesus left Judea and traveled north to the province of Galilee. There He would begin His great Galilean ministry of teaching, preaching, and healing (Matt. 4:23).

Settled in Capernaum (Matt. 4:13-14a). Although Jesus had lived for many years in Nazareth, He did not choose to make His hometown His base of operations. Along the Sea of Galilee lay Capernaum, a bustling town centered around the fishing industry. Capernaum became the headquarters for Jesus' Galilean ministry.

In the time of Jesus, Galilee was a vibrant commercial area. Several major roads crossed the region; so it saw a continual flow of people from throughout the Mediterranean world. Although Galileans were often ridiculed by the people of Judea, in reality they were much more involved in international life than were the inhabitants of Jerusalem. Galilee was thus an ideal location for Jesus to proclaim the good news.

—Daniel J. Estes.

QUESTIONS

1. What does the fact that the Spirit of God led Jesus into the wilderness tell us?
2. How did Jesus' physical condition make Him especially vulnerable to temptation?
3. Why did the devil encourage Jesus to use His power to turn stones into bread?
4. How did Jesus counter the devil's temptations?
5. How did the devil misuse Scripture in tempting Jesus?
6. What shortcut did the devil propose to Jesus for getting what rightfully belonged to Him?
7. Why was Jesus successful in overcoming Satan's attacks?
8. How did the angels help Jesus after His tests?
9. Why did Jesus leave Judea and go to Galilee?
10. Why was Galilee a strategic center for Jesus' early ministry?

—Daniel J. Estes.

PRACTICAL POINTS

1. God does not abandon us in times of temptation (Matt. 4:1; cf. I Cor. 10:13).
2. It is always a sin to pursue legitimate ends through illegitimate means (Matt. 4:2-3).
3. Our desire for God's Word should exceed even our desire for physical sustenance (vs. 4).
4. God's promises are not given to us so that we can test Him or show off our faith (vss. 5-7).
5. Let us be ever vigilant, for even the most godly people can be tempted by the worst sins (vss. 8-9).
6. God's Word, as it is known, understood, and consistently applied, is our best defense against Satan's temptations (vss. 10-11).
7. We must remember that the circumstances we encounter in life are God's way of fulfilling His plan for us (vss. 12-14).

—Jarl K. Waggoner.

RESEARCH AND DISCUSSION

1. How can we explain Matthew 4:1 in light of Jesus' teaching that we should pray that God not lead us into temptation (6:13)?
2. What does 4:2-9 tell us about the tactics Satan uses against believers? What does it reveal about the character of Christ?
3. Why was it necessary for Jesus to be tempted? How do we benefit from His temptation and His response to it (cf. Heb. 4:15)?
4. What are some ways that Christians can "tempt the Lord" (Matt. 4:7)?

—Jarl K. Waggoner.

Golden Text Illuminated

"But he answered and said, It is written, Man shall not live by bread alone, but by every word that proceedeth out of the mouth of God" (Matthew 4:4).

When John baptized Jesus, the Lord proclaimed His pleasure with His Son; immediately afterward, the Holy Spirit came to rest on Jesus as the Anointed One.

Now Jesus was compelled by that same Holy Spirit into the desert to fast and to endure temptations from Satan. This series of temptations was intended to prepare and confirm Jesus for the commencement of His earthly ministry. Unsurprisingly, Satan chose food as Jesus' first temptation. He must have reckoned this as foremost among Jesus' vulnerabilities at that time.

Satan's tactics have not changed since his temptation of Christ. He still tempts us wherever we are most vulnerable. But in contrast to Jesus, we often fall for his tricks. Nevertheless, we always have this promise from the apostle James: "Resist the devil, and he will flee from you" (4:7).

In resisting this particular temptation, Jesus quoted Deuteronomy 8:3. In doing so, He met Satan's earthly priorities with God's spiritual, heavenly ones. Jesus contended that God's Word is what is most essential, not physical food. Thus, He declined to use the power God had bestowed on Him for such a mundane purpose. God has already filled the earth with a bounty of earthly food, but Jesus' mission from the Father was to fill it with the spiritual food of God's Word!

—John Lody.

SCRIPTURE LESSON TEXT

JOHN 5:19 Then answered Jesus and said unto them, Verily, verily, I say unto you, The Son can do nothing of himself, but what he seeth the Father do: for what things soever he doeth, these also doeth the Son likewise.

20 For the Father loveth the Son, and sheweth him all things that himself doeth: and he will shew him greater works than these, that ye may marvel.

21 For as the Father raiseth up the dead, and quickeneth *them;* even so the Son quickeneth whom he will.

22 For the Father judgeth no man, but hath committed all judgment unto the Son:

23 That all *men* should honour the Son, even as they honour the Father. He that honoureth not the Son honoureth not the Father which hath sent him.

24 Verily, verily, I say unto you, He that heareth my word, and believeth on him that sent me, hath everlasting life, and shall not come into condemnation; but is passed from death unto life.

25 Verily, verily, I say unto you, The hour is coming, and now is, when the dead shall hear the voice of the Son of God: and they that hear shall live.

26 For as the Father hath life in himself; so hath he given to the Son to have life in himself;

27 And hath given him authority to execute judgment also, because he is the Son of man.

28 Marvel not at this: for the hour is coming, in the which all that are in the graves shall hear his voice,

29 And shall come forth; they that have done good, unto the resurrection of life; and they that have done evil, unto the resurrection of damnation.

NOTES

Doing the Father's Work

Lesson Text: John 5:19-29

Related Scriptures: Luke 2:41-52;
John 5:1-17; 8:25-30; 10:31-39; Philippians 2:5-11

TIME: A.D. 28   PLACE: Jerusalem

GOLDEN TEXT—"Verily, verily, I say unto you, He that heareth my word, and believeth on him that sent me, hath everlasting life, and shall not come into condemnation; but is passed from death unto life" (John 5:24).

Lesson Exposition

In John 5 we find Jesus making a visit to Jerusalem to attend a Jewish religious feast. He faced antagonism there, where He was not as popular as He was in Galilee. It began after He miraculously healed the man beside the pool of Bethesda who had been crippled for thirty-eight years (vs. 5).

Once the man told the Jewish leaders who had healed him, they determined to kill Jesus, primarily because He had done this work on the Sabbath (vs. 16). When they confronted Jesus, He told them that He was simply carrying on the work that His Father had been doing (vs. 17). That inflamed them even more. Now, He had made Himself equal to God.

THE FATHER AND THE SON— John 5:19-23

Their relationship (John 5:19-20). When Jesus said He was working just as His Father was working, He not only claimed equality with God, He also claimed to have the authority of God. Since the Jewish leaders considered His statement to be blasphemy, they believed He should be put to death. Jesus amplified His claim in verse 19

when He further based His authority on His relationship with God by saying He did everything the same way His Father did.

In the world of Jesus' day, the Romans ruled. To them, the Jews' religious activity meant little. To the Jews, the highest authority of all was their religion. Jesus was challenging them at the heart of their beliefs.

In the minds of the Jews in Jesus' day, the highest authority rested in their religious leaders. When Jesus explained His Sabbath actions on the basis of a higher authority than theirs, they reacted instantly and negatively.

Furthermore, Jesus claimed that God loved Him (His Son) and revealed to Him everything He was doing. This claim of unity meant that Jesus was doing only what God wanted done. In addition to that, Jesus said that He was going to do even greater things as God directed Him in the future.

Their ability to give life (John 5:21). The Jews believed God had the power to give life. He did so first at Creation but also at other times. For example, the prophet Elijah raised a widow's son to life after the boy had died (I Kgs. 17). Sometime later God did the same thing through Elijah's successor, Elisha (II Kgs. 4).

Perhaps the most interesting resurrection is the following: "And Elisha died, and they buried him. And the bands of the Moabites invaded the land at the coming in of the year. And it came to pass, as they were burying a man, that, behold, they spied a band of men; and they cast the man into the sepulchre of Elisha: and when the man was let down, and touched the bones of Elisha, he revived, and stood up on his feet" (II Kgs. 13:20-21).

Since the Jews were acquainted with the Old Testament Scriptures, they had no problem hearing that God can give life. They did have a big problem, however, when they heard Jesus say that He could also give life to whomever He chose. Once again, He claimed equality with God.

What is especially precious to us is the fact that Jesus gives spiritual as well as physical life. It is through Him that we can have eternal life.

Their handling of judgment (John 5:22-23). Jesus also claimed that the Father had conferred upon Him the authority to judge all things. He went so far as to say that the Father does not judge anyone but instead has committed all judgment to the Son. This also emphasizes the equality of Father and Son. Jesus stated that there is a reason the Father has committed all judgment to Him: that all should honor Him as they do the Father.

So important is it that people recognize Jesus' equality with His Father and His authority to judge that Jesus said anyone who does not honor the Son does not honor he Father either. The apostle Paul wrote in Philippians 2:9-11 that one day every knee will bow and acknowledge the supremacy of Jesus Christ.

PEOPLE AND THE SON—
John 5:24-29

Importance of belief (John 5:24-25). The Greek words that begin this paragraph are *amēn, amēn,* which has been translated, "verily, verily." It is intended to emphasize the certainty of the next statement. One might say, "I can tell you this with complete assurance of its truth." We are meant to pay special attention to what Jesus said next.

The truth Jesus stated is that anyone who hears His words and believes in the God who sent Him will be guaranteed eternal life, which will result in escape from judgment. Usually the wording of salvation truth emphasizes believing in Christ rather than in the Father. Since Jesus had been referring to His unity with the Father, it is understandable that He would say belief in the Father will result in eternal life.

The phrase "is passed from death unto life" (vs. 24) becomes even more important when we understand that in the Greek text, the perfect tense is used here. In this verse, that means a completed action took place sometime in the past and that it has continuing results. When we believed in Jesus Christ as our personal Saviour, we passed from death into life, and we remain there. When we believe in Jesus Christ, we become spiritually alive. At that moment of belief, we leave the realm of death and enter the realm of life. This spiritual life is also called everlasting life.

Once again Jesus stressed the certainty of His next remark: there would be a time—in fact, it had already begun—when the spiritually dead would hear His voice and live. This is the meaning we get from the little phrase "and now is" (vs. 25). The context is Jesus' ability to give life. The spiritually dead can hear and receive eternal life.

Authority for judgment (John 5:26-27). As humans, we do not have life in ourselves; we receive life from our Heavenly Father. He is life, and He is the source and Creator of all life. Jesus said the Father had given Him the same capacity. He has life in Himself and is not dependent upon any other source for life.

John's reason for recording this conversation of Jesus was probably his concern that his readers understand not only that Jesus possesses life in Himself but also that He has the power to give life to others. John 1:4 states, "In him was life; and the life was the light of men." It is the spiritual life that we receive from Jesus that gives us spiritual light, that is, understanding of God and His ways.

Not only was authority over life given to Jesus by His Father; so too was the authority to render judgment. God did this because Jesus is the Son of Man. The title emphasizes His human nature and is the one Jesus used most often in referring to Himself. It is especially meaningful to know that the judgments rendered will come from One who shared our human life.

Power for resurrection (John 5:28- 29). Here Jesus spoke of a future event, as opposed to what He seemed to refer to as something present in the phrase "and now is" in verse 25. There is a physical resurrection coming that will involve every person who has ever lived. There are, in fact, two resurrections mentioned in Jesus' words: a resurrection of life and a resurrection of damnation. The word translated "damnation" is the Greek word *krisis,* which refers to a tribunal at which justice according to divine law will be rendered. The first resurrection involves believers, that is, those who have a right relationship with God through His Son, Jesus. The second involves those who have not received Jesus Christ as Saviour. It will be a just judgment, for God is just (cf. Gen. 18:25).

In this text there is no distinction of time regarding the resurrections. Here Jesus referred only to the universality of resurrection. Everyone is going to face God at one time or another. Those who "have done good" (John 5:29) are those who have believed in Jesus and trusted Him for salvation. Goodness and good works do not earn heaven. Those who "have done evil" are those without Christ.

Perhaps no other passage in the Bible relays so effectively the seriousness of the decision we make regarding who Jesus is and what He came to do.

—Keith E. Eggert.

QUESTIONS

1. Why did the Jews become upset when Jesus said He was working in the same way as His Father?

2. Why did the Jews disagree with the idea that Jesus had authority from God higher than theirs?

3. Why did the Jews have no problem hearing that God gives life?

4. What makes it especially meaningful to us to know that Jesus gives life?

5. What did Jesus claim regarding His authority to judge?

6. Why did He say that it is important to recognize His equality with God?

7. What is the significance of Jesus' words "verily, verily" (John 5:24)?

8. What certain truth did Jesus state about believing in Him?

9. What takes place when people believe in Jesus Christ?

10. What did Jesus say about resurrection? Who is going to be there, and what are the destinations?

—Keith E. Eggert.

PRACTICAL POINTS

1. Just as Jesus was dependent on the Father, so we must recognize our dependence on Christ (John 5:19; cf. 15:5).
2. Our love for someone will be evident in our desire to share with that person (5:20).
3. The wonderful things Jesus did should prompt us to honor Him as God (vss. 21-23).
4. Because we cannot believe what we never hear, we must earnestly study the words of Christ (vs. 24).
5. Life—natural, spiritual, and eternal—is a precious gift from God (vss. 25-26).
6. The judgment after death is as certain as death itself (John 5:27-29; cf. Heb. 9:27).

—Ralph Woodworth.

RESEARCH AND DISCUSSION

1. Why could Jesus not do anything without the Father (John 5:19)?
2. What are some of the greater things the Son would do that would cause the people to marvel (vs. 20)?
3. If the Son could not do anything without the Father, why was He given the responsibility of judging (vs. 22)?
4. What are some things we can do to honor the Son (vs. 23)?
5. If everlasting life comes from hearing and believing, can those who have no opportunity to hear be saved (vss. 24-25)?
6. What qualifies Jesus to execute judgment (vs. 27)?

—Ralph Woodworth.

Golden Text Illuminated

"Verily, verily, I say unto you, He that heareth my word, and believeth on him that sent me, hath everlasting life, and shall not come into condemnation; but is passed from death unto life" (John 5:24).

Our golden text begins with a double *amēn* (in the original), which is translated "Verily, verily," meaning "Truly, truly." Every word Jesus spoke is important but when Jesus says, "Verily, verily," the reader/hearer should pay special attention.

What Jesus wants any and all to know is that it is extremely urgent to hear what He has to say. To hear means not only to hear with the ear but also to be obedient to the words one hears.

The way to receive the gift of life from Jesus is the way of faith. One must hear His word and believe Jesus was sent from God as the One the Scriptures promised would come.

To hear His word and believe (obey) is to receive everlasting life. The life Jesus gives comes at the time of belief. That is clear by the statement that there is no condemnation in the future for the believer (cf. Rom. 8:1). Jesus stated that the believer has already passed over from death to life. That is the present case for believers, but it has future implications. The believer will not come into judgment on the last day, either.

It is a blessing to be among those who have heard the Word of God and, with sorrowful repentance for sin, embraced Him. For the believer, that was his judgment day and the day when everlasting life was imparted. Because of this, we should honor Christ with our worship.

—Darrell W. McKay.

SCRIPTURE LESSON TEXT

MATT. 26:36 Then cometh Jesus with them unto a place called Gethsemane, and saith unto the disciples, Sit ye here, while I go and pray yonder.

37 And he took with him Peter and the two sons of Zebedee, and began to be sorrowful and very heavy.

38 Then saith he unto them, My soul is exceeding sorrowful, even unto death: tarry ye here, and watch with me.

39 And he went a little further, and fell on his face, and prayed, saying, O my Father, if it be possible, let this cup pass from me: nevertheless not as I will, but as thou *wilt*.

40 And he cometh unto the disciples, and findeth them asleep, and saith unto Peter, What, could ye not watch with me one hour?

41 Watch and pray, that ye enter not into temptation: the spirit indeed *is* willing, but the flesh *is* weak.

42 He went away again the second time, and prayed, saying, O my Father, if this cup may not pass away from me, except I drink it, thy will be done.

43 And he came and found them asleep again: for their eyes were heavy.

44 And he left them, and went away again, and prayed the third time, saying the same words.

45 Then cometh he to his disciples, and saith unto them, Sleep on now, and take *your* rest: behold, the hour is at hand, and the Son of man is betrayed into the hands of sinners.

46 Rise, let us be going: behold, he is at hand that doth betray me.

47 And while he yet spake, lo, Judas, one of the twelve, came, and with him a great multitude with swords and staves, from the chief priests and elders of the people.

48 Now he that betrayed him gave them a sign, saying, Whomsoever I shall kiss, that same is he: hold him fast.

49 And forthwith he came to Jesus, and said, Hail, master; and kissed him.

50 And Jesus said unto him, Friend, wherefore art thou come? Then came they, and laid hands on Jesus, and took him.

NOTES

Submitting to the Father's Will

Lesson Text: Matthew 26:36-50

Related Scriptures: Psalm 88:1-18; Mark 14:32-42;
John 12:20-26; Hebrews 5:7-9

TIME: A.D. 30   PLACE: Mount of Olives

GOLDEN TEXT—"And he went a little further, and fell on his face, and prayed, saying, O my Father, if it be possible, let this cup pass from me: nevertheless not as I will, but as thou wilt" (Matthew 26:39).

Lesson Exposition

FIRST PRAYER—Matt. 26:36-41

Rest (Matt. 26:36). Judas was familiar with the Garden of Gethsemane and knew that Jesus and His disciples were likely to make their way there that night.

Jesus instructed the disciples to sit in a certain location while He withdrew to another spot for a session of prayer. They probably thought that He expected them to serve as watchmen and warn Him if anyone hostile appeared. This would be one form of rest from the exertions of the day.

Request (Matt. 26:37-38). Jesus took His inner circle of Peter, James, and John with Him to another location. A mood of heavy sorrow enveloped Jesus. He told these three men that His soul was exceedingly sorrowful, even to the point of threatening death.

It would appear that Jesus wanted Peter, James, and John to be with Him and lend their support to Him as His time of suffering approached. This certainly was a reasonable request of His three closest disciples.

Resignation (Matt. 26:39). Jesus went about a stone's throw away from the three disciples (Luke 22:41). There He knelt down and, according to Matthew's account, fell on His face to pray. Addressing God as His Father, Jesus asked that, if possible, the cup He was about to drink might be taken away from Him. However, He was prepared to do God's will. He was submissive, surrendered, and acquiescent as an obedient Son.

In considering what the cup represented, we are faced with at least two possibilities. One is that Jesus wanted to avoid enduring the shame and agony of a mock trial, cruel torture, and excruciating crucifixion.

The more likely reason for Jesus' agony in the garden is that He was contemplating the awful prospect of enduring the wrath of His heavenly Father as He bore the sins of mankind.

Rebuke (Matt. 26:40-41). After His first prayer, Jesus returned to Peter, James, and John. He found the three men sleeping. Waking Peter, Jesus expressed disappointment that he could not stay awake to watch for even one hour. By this time the two sons of Zebedee also may have been awake to hear the rebuke and to share in it.

Although Jesus did not mention it to Peter, James, and John, He had been visited by an angel after His first prayer and strengthened by him (Luke 22:43). Jesus had been helped by a heavenly being when He had been deprived of the help requested from His earthly companions.

Jesus now urged His disciples to watch and pray so that they would not fall into temptation and suffer the consequences of it. He wanted them to be prepared for what was coming so that they would not yield to temptation. It was one thing to have a willing spirit, but it was another thing to restrain the weakness of their flesh. Paul later considered this topic when he dealt with the continual struggle of the Spirit with the flesh (Rom. 7:15— 8:13). The only way to be victorious is to live by the power of the Holy Spirit.

SECOND PRAYER—Matt. 26:42-43

Repetition (Matt. 26:42). No response to Jesus by the three disciples is recorded. We assume that they felt chastened, but as subsequent verses show, they were apparently so exhausted that they could not stay awake to profit from what He said.

Jesus moved back to His place of prayer and repeated the request He had made about the cup passing from Him; at least, that is what seems to be implied. His emphasis now, however, was on resignation to do His Father's will if He had to drink from that cup.

Repose (Matt. 26:43). Jesus returned to the place where Peter, James, and John were located. He found them again in repose, their eyes heavy with sleep. This time it seems He gave them no rebuke. He understood the limitations of their human frames and was not willing to scold them again.

THIRD PRAYER—Matt. 26:44-46

Repetition (Matt. 26:44). Jesus moved back to His place of prayer and repeated the request He had made before, saying the same words. His willingness to do His Father's will remained constant.

If the divine Son of God felt it was appropriate to repeat the same prayer three times, there may be a lesson in this for us. God expects all of His children to be persistent in making their requests known to Him. The important thing is that they be ready to accept His answers of "yes," "no," or "wait." It is God's will that is vital, not our own will (I John 5:14-15).

Resignation (Matt. 26:45-46). Jesus' resignation to His Father was next transposed to resignation to the situation with His disciples. He returned to Peter, James, and John and again found them sleeping, as were the other eight disciples at their location. Jesus told them to sleep on now and take their rest.

Thus we see a threefold resignation on Jesus' part. First, He was resigned to God's will. Second, He was resigned to His disciples' exhaustion. Third, He was resigned to His betrayal and arrest. Once we have resigned ourselves to God's will, we are ready to resign ourselves to whatever else is necessary in order to carry it out.

BETRAYAL—Matt. 26:47-50

Plan (Matt. 26:47-48). If it appears that Jesus was aware of the approach of Judas and the multitude of people accompanying him, that is exactly right. Before the sounds of their approach could be heard by the disciples, Jesus knew they were coming. He even knew what was in the minds and hearts of men (John 2:25).

Judas Iscariot had given the multitude a sign, saying that the one he kissed in greeting would be Jesus. They were to grab Him and hold Him fast. This was the plan, and it was put into motion. It might be noted here that affectionate gestures such as this between men were common to the culture and customs of that time. In fact, men in the Middle East still have a habit of greeting one another with a kiss and even walking together hand in hand without any sexual overtones.

Perfidy (Matt. 26:49-50). We can find more details of this incident in John 18:2-13. "Jesus therefore, knowing all things that should come upon him, went forth, and said unto them, Whom seek ye? They answered him, Jesus of Nazareth. Jesus saith unto them, I am he. . . . As soon then as he had said unto them, I am he, they went backward, and fell to the ground."

Jesus again asked them for whom they sought. They told Him it was Jesus of Nazareth, and He repeated His statement that He was that person. Then He requested that His disciples be allowed to go free.

In spite of the fact that Jesus had identified Himself twice to the arresting mob, Judas came up to Him to hail, or greet, Him as Master and to kiss Him.

Peter's action in cutting off the right ear of Malchus, the high priest's servant, was rebuked by Jesus. He told him to put his sword back into his sheath, remarking that those who take to the sword will perish by the sword. Jesus could have prayed to His Father and had twelve legions of angels come to rescue Him from the arresting mob, but then the Scriptures regarding His atoning death would not have been fulfilled (Matt. 26:51-54).

The incident regarding Peter's rash act with his sword is mentioned here because it ties in directly with the cup Jesus was destined to drink as recorded in our lesson text. "Then said Jesus unto Peter, Put up thy sword into the sheath: the cup which my Father hath given me, shall I not drink it?" (John 18:11).

The evil deed was done. The captain and officers of the Jews took hold of Jesus and bound Him (John 18:12). They led Him away to the high priest's house.

One of the saddest reports in the Bible is this: "Then all the disciples forsook him, and fled" (Matt. 26:56; cf. Mark 14:50). They would go into hiding until after Christ's resurrection, after He appeared to them. They would not begin their work until after they were empowered by the Holy Spirit to go out and begin changing the world. If the Spirit can make that kind of transformation in them, He can do the same for us.

—*Gordon Talbot.*

QUESTIONS

1. What did Jesus tell His disciples to do in the Garden of Gethsemane?

2. How sorrowful did Jesus tell Peter, James, and John He was?

3. What likely was the cup that Jesus was reluctant to drink?

4. How did Jesus receive strength after His first prayer?

5. Why did Jesus tell His sleepy disciples to watch and pray?

6. What does Jesus' example in repeating His prayer teach us?

7. What three types of resignation did Jesus display in Gethsemane?

8. When did Jesus know that Judas and the mob were coming?

9. How did Judas plan to betray Jesus to the multitude?

10. In what way did all the disciples let Jesus down?

—*Gordon Talbot.*

PRACTICAL POINTS

1. Experiencing emotional turmoil can prepare us to minister to others (Matt. 26:36-38; cf. Heb. 4:15-16).
2. Submissive obedience is a mark of Christlikeness (Matt. 26:39).
3. The discipline of prayer is demanding, but it is necessary for overcoming temptation (vss. 40-41).
4. Do not hesitate to repeat heartfelt prayers (vss. 42-44).
5. A time of spiritual rest is necessary to prepare Christ's followers for a time of spiritual battle (vss. 45-46).
6. Spiritual betrayal is no coincidence; it always involves a definite plan of action (vss. 47-48).
7. Not everyone who calls Jesus "Master" will enter His kingdom (26:49-50; cf. 7:21-23).

—Thomas R. Chmura.

RESEARCH AND DISCUSSION

1. How important is it to have a spiritual accountability partner, and what level of intimacy should you strive for (Matt. 26:36-38)?
2. What does verse 39 reveal concerning the perfect humanity of Jesus Christ?
3. What type of spiritual exercise and discipline will combat the dangers of spiritual lethargy (Matt. 26:40-41; cf. Eph. 5:14-17)?
4. What does Christ's response to His disciples' repeated weakness teach you about His compassionate grace (Matt. 26:42-45)?
5. What is at the heart of spiritual hypocrisy (vss. 48-49)?

—Thomas R. Chmura.

Golden Text Illuminated

"And he went a little further, and fell on his face, and prayed, saying, O my Father, if it be possible, let this cup pass from me: nevertheless not as I will, but as thou wilt" (Matthew 26:39).

Our golden text records the first of Jesus' three prayers in the garden, all of similar content: He asked the Father to let the cup of His impending torture and crucifixion pass from Him if possible, followed by His affirmation of willingness to do His Father's will, no matter what.

Jesus' resolve to do His Father's will is a shining example for us. Jesus was as frail and human as any of us, yet He relied upon the power of God through the Holy Spirit to overcome His human weakness and give Himself as an offering for our redemption.

We have the same spiritual resources available to us today that Jesus relied on that fateful night in Gethsemane. But will we trust our heavenly Father's will for us as He did?

Even with the Holy Spirit dwelling inside us, our fallen human nature craves autonomy. We stubbornly desire to maintain a firm grasp on the tiller of our own destiny, no matter how many times we have experienced the Father's faithfulness.

Yet Jesus forsook His own welfare for the sake of those He loved. He chose to keep His own will in perfect sync with the will of His heavenly Father so that He could redeem us from our lost condition.

To truly follow Jesus' example in Gethsemane, we must love God and others enough to trust His will under the most extreme and demanding situations.

—John Lody.

SCRIPTURE LESSON TEXT

MATT. 27:38 Then were there two thieves crucified with him, one on the right hand, and another on the left.

39 And they that passed by reviled him, wagging their heads,

40 And saying, Thou that destroyest the temple, and buildest *it* in three days, save thyself. If thou be the Son of God, come down from the cross.

41 Likewise also the chief priests mocking *him,* with the scribes and elders, said,

42 He saved others; himself he cannot save. If he be the King of Israel, let him now come down from the cross, and we will believe him.

43 He trusted in God; let him deliver him now, if he will have him: for he said, I am the Son of God.

44 The thieves also, which were crucified with him, cast the same in his teeth.

45 Now from the sixth hour there was darkness over all the land unto the ninth hour.

46 And about the ninth hour Jesus cried with a loud voice, saying, Eli, Eli, lama sabachthani? that is to say, My God, my God, why hast thou forsaken me?

47 Some of them that stood there, when they heard *that,* said, This *man* calleth for Elias.

48 And straightway one of them ran, and took a spunge, and filled *it* with vinegar, and put *it* on a reed, and gave him to drink.

49 The rest said, Let be, let us see whether Elias will come to save him.

50 Jesus, when he had cried again with a loud voice, yielded up the ghost.

51 And, behold, the veil of the temple was rent in twain from the top to the bottom; and the earth did quake, and the rocks rent;

52 And the graves were opened; and many bodies of the saints which slept arose,

53 And came out of the graves after his resurrection, and went into the holy city, and appeared unto many.

54 Now when the centurion, and they that were with him, watching Jesus, saw the earthquake, and those things that were done, they feared greatly, saying, Truly this was the Son of God.

NOTES

Crucified for Sinners

Lesson Text: Matthew 27:38-54

Related Scriptures: Psalm 22:1-18; Isaiah 53:3-12; Luke 23:32-47

TIME: A.D. 30   PLACE: Golgotha

GOLDEN TEXT—"We have seen and do testify that the Father sent the Son to be the Saviour of the world" (I John 4:14).

Lesson Exposition

ABUSE OF JESUS—Matt. 27:38-44

Crucified among criminals (Matt. 27:38). Matthew 26 and 27 trace the sad series of events that brought Jesus to the cross. Jesus was betrayed by Judas, arrested by an armed force sent by the Jewish leaders, illegally convicted by the Jewish court, and then condemned to death by the intimidated governor. He was subjected to abuse, taunting, beating, and total injustice as He died on the cross.

Jesus was not the only man condemned to die that day. Along with Him were two others. They are called "thieves" (vs. 38). The term Matthew used to describe them most likely refers to individuals guilty of political rebellion against the Roman government. It may well have been that Barabbas was scheduled for execution that day as well, because he also was a robber, or insurrectionist (cf. John 18:40). He was released by Pilate at the insistence of the multitude, and Jesus may have taken his place on the cross (Matt. 27:15-26).

Scorned by spectators (Matt. 27:39-40). The Romans chose public places for crucifixions. They wanted this terrible display of death to deter other people from crime. They were ruthless rulers.

No doubt word about Jesus' arrest and conviction had passed quickly through the city. Among the charges brought against Jesus was that He had said that He was able to destroy the temple and to rebuild it in three days (26:61).

The spectators who were present at the crucifixion were scornful to Jesus. They knew that He had claimed to be the Son of God, so they called on Him to save Himself by coming down from the cross. Little did they realize that they were echoing the words of Satan (Matt. 4:3, 6) as they challenged Jesus to prove His deity.

Mocked by religious leaders (Matt. 27:41-43). Joining with the scornful spectators, the religious leaders mocked Jesus. They were filled with envy and hate.

The leaders took words that Jesus had spoken and threw them back in His face. Jesus had claimed to save others, but He could not save Himself. He had claimed to be the King of Israel; if He came down from the cross, they would believe Him, they said. He called Himself the Son of God, but where was

God when Jesus needed His help?

Throughout His ministry Jesus was opposed by the religious leaders. Even as He was dying for the sins of the world, they insisted on mocking the Saviour. They did not recognize and respond to His love for them.

Insulted by thieves (Matt. 27:44). The final voices in the choir of abuse against Jesus came from the two thieves, or insurrectionists. Even in the pain of their crucifixion, they too insulted Jesus.

ABANDONMENT OF JESUS— Matt. 27:45-50

Suffering in darkness (Matt. 27:45). Jesus was placed on the cross at the third hour (Mark 15:25), or nine o'clock in the morning. After He had suffered there for three hours, supernatural darkness descended upon the land until three o'clock in the afternoon.

This could not have been a solar eclipse, because the Passover was always held at the full moon, making an eclipse impossible. Instead, it was a supernatural darkening of the skies by God. In the eerie daytime darkness, Jesus suffered on the cross as He bore the sins of the world.

Suffering in loneliness (Matt. 27:46-47). Although there was a crowd watching His crucifixion, Jesus felt alone and abandoned. Quoting the words of Psalm 22:1, Jesus cried out, "My God, my God, why hast thou forsaken me?"

Theologians have long struggled to fully understand what these words mean. How could God the Father forsake God the Son? In bearing the sins of the world, Jesus became sin for us (II Cor. 5:21). He was made a curse for us (Gal. 3:13). In a way that defies human understanding and surpasses human language, Jesus as the sin-Bearer was alienated from fellowship with God the Father. To be our Substitute, He had to endure the unspeakable pain of being forsaken by His Father. There is no way that we can appreciate the full import of what this meant for Jesus.

"Eli," which means "my God" (Matt. 27:46), sounds much like the name of the great Old Testament prophet Elijah. Some of the bystanders thought that Jesus was calling out to Elijah.

Suffering in ridicule (Matt. 27:48-49). Hearing Jesus' cry, one of the people, most likely one of the soldiers, filled a sponge with sour, vinegary liquid and lifted it to Jesus to give Him a drink. This beverage was the common drink of soldiers and poor people, so it was readily available. It was an act of individual kindness to Jesus as He suffered intensely.

The rest of the crowd, however, did not manifest even the minimum of human sensitivity toward one in great pain. In their hostile opposition to Jesus, they told the person who had been kind to Him to stop. With scornful skepticism they said, "Let us see whether Elias (Elijah) will come to save him" (vs. 49). Even in the presence of Jesus' excruciating pain, they insisted on ridiculing Him. They sought to halt the one person who offered some help, and they only added to Jesus' suffering by their sarcastic words.

Suffering in death (Matt. 27:50). Crucifixion was a horrible form of execution calculated to prolong the agony of death.

Typically, crucifixion resulted in profound exhaustion. Jesus, however, was in control of His faculties even when on the cross. At the ninth hour, around three o'clock in the afternoon, He cried again with a loud voice. This was not the feeble whimper of a defeated victim but rather the triumphant cry of the Victor: "It is finished" (John 19:30).

Jesus had willingly laid down His life as the sacrifice for human sins. That accomplished, He voluntarily yielded up His spirit, or "ghost" (Matt. 27:50). His death was not a tragedy in which Jesus was defeated by evil men; it was His conscious, intentional triumph over sin.

ACKNOWLEDGEMENT OF JESUS—Matt. 27:51-54

The torn veil (Matt. 27:51a). Although Jesus had been crucified as though He were a common criminal, several events at the time of His death testified to the truth that He was indeed the Son of God. At Jesus' death the veil in the temple was torn from top to bottom. That the tear began at the top suggests that God Himself was responsible.

The temple veil had barred the way to the Holy of Holies, which represented the presence of God. In the Old Testament system, only the high priest could enter the Holy of Holies, and then only on the Day of Atonement with the blood of the atonement offering for the nation.

Hebrews 10:19-20 develops the significance of the torn veil. By His death, Jesus opened up direct access to God. Instead of going through the Old Testament priesthood, Christians now can enter boldly into the presence of God through the blood of Jesus.

The opened tombs (Matt. 27:51b-53). When Jesus died, the earth was shaken by a powerful earthquake. Rocks were torn apart as God's mighty power was displayed. In ancient Israel, tombs were usually caves hewn in the stone, with rocks placed over the entrances. It was not surprising, therefore, that the earthquake caused many tombs to open.

What was astonishing, however, was that after Jesus' resurrection, the bodies of many believers were resur-rected. They came out of their graves, went into Jerusalem, and appeared to many people there. What an incredible sight that must have been!

The convinced centurion (Matt. 27:54). The Roman centurion and his band of soldiers had no doubt performed numerous crucifixions. Jesus' death, however, was vastly different from all others they had witnessed. They heard the bystanders and the religious leaders mock Jesus because He claimed to be the Son of God (vss. 40, 43). As they watched the way in which Jesus died and as they experienced the earthquake, they became terrified. They could only conclude that Jesus truly was the Son of God.

—Daniel J. Estes.

QUESTIONS

1. Who was crucified alongside Jesus?
2. How did the people who were passing by use Jesus' words to scorn Him?
3. How did the religious leaders mock Jesus?
4. For how long did Jesus suffer in darkness?
5. Why was Jesus forsaken by God the Father?
6. How did one man demonstrate compassion to Jesus in His pain?
7. How did the spectators ridicule Jesus' cry to the Father?
8. How did the rending of the temple veil symbolize the significance of Jesus' death?
9. What happened when the earthquake opened many graves?
10. How did the Roman soldiers respond to Jesus' death?

—Daniel J. Estes.

PRACTICAL POINTS

1. It was entirely appropriate that our Saviour died the death of a criminal, since He was dying for violators of God's law (Matt. 27:38).
2. We must not allow mockery to shake our faith; it is merely an attempt by the wicked to justify their own unbelief (vss. 39-44).
3. The suffering Christ endured should remind us of the depth of our sin before God (vss. 45-46).
4. The most heartfelt expressions of God's people will often be ridiculed and mocked by the enemies of Christ (vss. 47-49).
5. Jesus' life was not taken from Him; He freely gave His life so that we can have everlasting life (Matt. 27:50; cf. John 10:15-18).
6. Christ's death guarantees the believer both free access to God and future resurrection unto eternal life (Matt. 27:51-54).

—Jarl K. Waggoner.

RESEARCH AND DISCUSSION

1. Why did Jesus suffer the great indignities He experienced on the cross (Matt. 27:38-44)?
2. What accounts for the hateful behavior of those who witnessed Jesus' crucifixion? How is such hatred of Christ exhibited today in the world around us?
3. What does a knowledge of Psalm 22 contribute to our understanding of Jesus' suffering and death?
4. Why is it important doctrinally to note that Jesus willingly gave His life on the cross (Matt. 27:50)?

—Jarl K. Waggoner.

Golden Text Illuminated

"We have seen and do testify that the Father sent the Son to be the Saviour of the world" (I John 4:14).

To whom does the "we" in the golden text refer? It "certainly refers to all those, especially the apostles, who had direct knowledge of Jesus' earthly life; but it probably ought not to be limited to them" (Gaebelein, ed., *The Expositor's Bible Commentary,* Zondervan).

There indeed was eyewitness testimony to the life, death, burial, and resurrection of Jesus Christ. The word "sent" also indicates that Jesus was a historical person.

Christ really lived in time and history. Those things that took place as described in our Scripture lesson, as well as in the other Gospels, were historical and real.

This being said, we still must consider the possibility that "the first person plural in verses 7-13 is . . . meant to include the readers" (Walvoord and Zuck, eds., *The Bible Knowledge Commentary,* Victor).

Although no one has "seen God at any time" (I John 4:12), the believer does, in a sense, see by faith.

Because the Holy Spirit in us gives us this seeing experience, we are to "testify" to the truth of the gospel.

The value of Christ's death is found in who He was and is—the Son of God. He was the only one who could save us.

Jesus' mission was "to seek and to save that which was lost" (Luke 19:10). He commissions all believers to tell everyone this good news!

—Richard P. Voth.

SCRIPTURE LESSON TEXT

JOHN 20:1 The first *day* of the week cometh Mary Magdalene early, when it was yet dark, unto the sepulchre, and seeth the stone taken away from the sepulchre.

2 Then she runneth, and cometh to Simon Peter, and to the other disciple, whom Jesus loved, and saith unto them, They have taken away the Lord out of the sepulchre, and we know not where they have laid him.

3 Peter therefore went forth, and that other disciple, and came to the sepulchre.

4 So they ran both together: and the other disciple did outrun Peter, and came first to the sepulchre.

5 And he stooping down, *and looking in,* saw the linen clothes lying; yet went he not in.

6 Then cometh Simon Peter following him, and went into the sepulchre, and seeth the linen clothes lie,

7 And the napkin, that was about his head, not lying with the linen clothes, but wrapped together in a place by itself.

8 Then went in also that other disciple, which came first to the sepulchre, and he saw, and believed.

9 For as yet they knew not the scripture, that he must rise again from the dead.

10 Then the disciples went away again unto their own home.

19 Then the same day at evening, being the first *day* of the week, when the doors were shut where the disciples were assembled for fear of the Jews, came Jesus and stood in the midst, and saith unto them, Peace *be* unto you.

20 And when he had so said, he shewed unto them *his* hands and his side. Then were the disciples glad, when they saw the Lord.

NOTES

Adult Bible Class   29

Risen from the Dead!
(Easter)

Lesson Text: John 20:1-10, 19-20

Related Scriptures: Psalm 16:1-11; Luke 24:1-12;
I Corinthians 15:12-19; Ephesians 1:15-23

TIME: A.D. 30   PLACES: near Jerusalem; Jerusalem

GOLDEN TEXT—"Then the same day at evening, being the first day of the week, when the doors were shut where the disciples were assembled for fear of the Jews, came Jesus and stood in the midst, and saith unto them, Peace be unto you" (John 20:19).

Lesson Exposition

THE UNEXPECTED EMPTY TOMB—John 20:1-5

The discovery (John 20:1). While John focused on Mary Magdalene in his Gospel, the other authors tell us she was not alone in going to the tomb on that first day of the week. Matthew 28:1 says "the other Mary" went with her. Mark 16:1 includes Mary the mother of James as present. This is probably who Matthew refers to. Mark also mentions Salome, who was the mother of James and John and the wife of Zebedee. Mary Magdalene had been a loyal follower of Jesus for a long time because He had cast seven demons out of her (Luke 8:2)

The last the women had seen, the tomb had been closed with a large stone over the entryway. According to Mark 16:3, they were having a discussion on the way to the tomb that morning: "And they said among themselves, Who shall roll us away the stone from the door of the sepulchre?" We understand their concern when Mark mentions that "when they looked, they saw that the stone was rolled away: for it

was very great" (vs. 4). Their discovery of the open entryway was both a surprise and a relief at first, being completely unexpected.

Matthew explains why the stone was rolled away: "And, behold, there was a great earthquake: for the angel of the Lord descended from heaven, and came and rolled back the stone from the door, and sat upon it" (28:2). John does not indicate that Mary saw the angel at this time. She must have arrived first, taken an initial look, and then left immediately to tell the disciples before the other women arrived. She returned later and was the first one to see Jesus alive when He made a special appearance to her at the tomb (John 20:14).

The report (John 20:2-3). Mary immediately ran to find Simon Peter and John ("the other disciple, whom Jesus loved" [cf. 19:26]). Her initial evaluation of the situation was that someone had taken the body of Jesus to another location. Even though Jesus had often spoken of the fact that He would rise from death, she had never really grasped that, so she had no thoughts about that possibility now.

The other women who followed Mary to the tomb entered it and found Jesus' body gone and two angels present who announced His resurrection (Luke 24:4-7). These women also hurried off to report these things to the disciples (vss. 9-10). However, according to Luke, the women's words seemed to the disciples "as idle tales, and they believed them not" (vs. 11). But it did not take long for Peter to decide to look into their story (vs. 12), and John decided to go too (John 20:3). They would naturally be concerned if the body of Jesus had been removed and taken somewhere else. These two were the most likely candidates for checking things out: the leader of the group and Jesus' beloved friend John.

The follow-up (John 20:4-5). The two disciples were off on a footrace. While Peter, the older one, left first, John, the youngest of all the disciples, not surprisingly soon overtook him and arrived at the tomb ahead of Peter. What might be a little surprising is that John did not enter the tomb right away but merely leaned over and looked in. We are not told whether he was fearful or just hesitant because of the unique and unexpected situation he was facing. For whatever reason, he waited until Peter arrived.

When John looked into the tomb, he saw the linen clothes in which Jesus had been buried. This is one of the evidences that His body had not been stolen, for no thief or person moving a body to another location would have taken time to unwrap it. This should have been an immediate reassurance to John that something other than that had occurred. There was no evidence of any type of crime, and the graveclothes were lying there empty. They were lying there looking like Jesus must have simply passed through them!

THE GRADUALLY EXPANDED UNDERSTANDING— John 20:6-10, 19-20

Seeing the burial clothes (John 20:6-7). When Peter arrived, he did a typical "Peter thing." He never hesitated to act or speak and often got himself in trouble because of it. So when he got to the tomb, he walked right in without hesitation. There he saw what John had seen when he peered in from the outside: the linen wrappings were neatly lying there in the place where Jesus' body had been. Now there were two eyewitnesses to the fact that the clothes had been left behind without a body in them.

"Whether motivated by shame or just acting according to character, Peter plunged into the darkness. We assume one of the men carried some kind of lantern or torch. The text says that Peter saw what John had seen and in addition, the burial cloth. But the word changes to one with a slightly different meaning, perhaps best translated as 'noticed' rather than 'looked at'" (Gangel, *Holman New Testament Commentary: John,* Broadman & Holman).

Believing the evidence (John 20:8-10). Matthew 20:17-19 says, "And Jesus going up to Jerusalem took the twelve disciples apart in the way, and said unto them, Behold, we go up to Jerusalem; and the Son of man shall be betrayed unto the chief priests and unto the scribes, and they shall condemn him to death, and shall deliver him to the Gentiles to mock, and to scourge, and to crucify him: and the third day he shall rise again." While Jesus said this on several occasions, the disciples somehow failed to grasp His words.

Later, the disciples became so focused on what Jesus was facing in His crucifixion that the promise of His resurrection to follow was completely forgotten or ignored. John finally understood when he followed Peter into the empty tomb. When he saw the whole scene, including the headpiece lying there by itself, he finally grasped the truth of what Jesus had said about the resurrection. He believed as he looked upon the empty tomb. Up to that point in time, the disciples had not comprehended the truth about the resurrection.

"So three of Jesus' followers saw the empty tomb, but John was not finished with his report. He wanted his readers to know that after Peter entered the tomb, John himself finally found enough courage to follow him. Now we have yet another use of the English verb *saw* and yet a third Greek word appearing in the original text. This time John uses a word that means 'to perceive with understanding.' That is why our text reads that John *saw and believed*" (Gangel). It must have been an exciting moment!

Showing the wounds (John 20:19-20). It was still the same day when Jesus made this appearance to His disciples, but it was now evening. This is reiterated in the statement that it was the first day of the week. The disciples had met and were in hiding because they feared the Jewish leaders who had seen to Jesus' crucifixion.

Suddenly, Jesus was standing there among them. His new resurrection body no longer maintained the limitations His body previously had. Apparently this sudden appearance terrified the disciples, for Jesus immediately spoke words of peace to them. They had never before seen anything like this happen and had no concept of the nature of a resurrected body; this sudden, unexpected appearance would have completely unsettled them. We can only imagine the rapid change of emotions that coursed through them in those brief moments.

Jesus further assured them by demonstrating that His was a material body. He had them look at His hands and side to see the wounds there. He wanted them to know for certain that they were not looking at a ghost or anything to be feared. This was immediately reassuring, and their emotions were soon those of gladness.

"The historical fact of the resurrection and its theological meaning will become the centerpiece of apostolic preaching in the Book of Acts. Perhaps from impetus provided by Peter and John, New Testament preachers claimed that the Savior is forever alive—a dramatic truth of the heart of the gospel to this very day. Our living Lord has conquered both sin and death. We can function in spite of trouble and heartache, knowing the ultimate victory is his and ours" (Gangel).
—Keith E. Eggert.

QUESTIONS

1. On which of the women who went to Jesus' tomb on resurrection morning did John focus?
2. Why was she so loyal to Jesus?
3. What did Mary immediately do after she arrived at the tomb?
4. What was the disciples' initial response to what the women told them?
5. Who decided to check out their story, and what did they do when they arrived at the tomb?
6. What did these men find at the tomb?
7. What was it that led to John's belief in the resurrection?
8. When after His resurrection did Jesus appear to His disciples?
9. How did He reassure them that He was in a material body?
10. Why did Jesus want His disciples to be assured in this way?
—Keith E. Eggert.

PRACTICAL POINTS

1. Those who serve God with great love will be first to witness His greatest wonders (John 20:1).
2. Those who love Christ are eager to be witnesses to His resurrection and salvation (vss. 2-4).
3. Some people believe after much contemplation; others believe right away (vss. 5-8).
4. No matter how well we know the Bible, God always brings forth fresh truths as we reread and meditate upon it (vss. 9-10).
5. In the midst of our worst fears and troubles, Jesus is with us, offering us His peace (vs. 19).
6. To be in the presence of Jesus is the highest joy (vs. 20)!

—John Lody.

RESEARCH AND DISCUSSION

1. John's Gospel tells us that Mary Magdalene was the first to visit Jesus' tomb, early that morning. Using commentaries and harmonies of the Gospels, can you discover the actual order of events on that first Easter morning?
2. Are you enthusiastic about Christ's resurrection this Easter season? How can you personally be an enthusiastic witness?
3. Read the four Gospel accounts of Christ's resurrection. Share with your Sunday school class the new insights impressed upon you.
4. God's comfort for you is meant to also comfort others (cf. II Cor. 1:4). How has God comforted you in the midst of your fears and trials?

—John Lody.

Golden Text Illuminated

"Then the same day at evening, being the first day of the week, when the doors were shut where the disciples were assembled for fear of the Jews, came Jesus and stood in the midst, and saith unto them, Peace be unto you" (John 20:19).

Our golden text takes place on the evening of resurrection Sunday. The disciples had hidden themselves behind closed doors because they feared the Jewish leaders.

Into this atmosphere of intense trepidation, Jesus Himself suddenly appears in their midst, greeting them in peace.

The resurrection of Christ is the vindication of all His redemptive work on behalf of all who trust Him as Lord and Saviour. It is God's stamp of approval on our salvation from sin.

Without the resurrection, our faith is meaningless. As Paul writes, "If Christ be not risen, then is our preaching vain, and your faith is also vain. . . . If in this life only we have hope in Christ, we are of all men most miserable" (I Cor. 15:14, 19).

Yet this is precisely what modern skepticism advocates. It contends that we must jettison all supernatural elements, including the resurrection, and live merely to follow Christ's moral example.

But what would be the value in following Christ's example if His redemptive work were a failure? If we pursued such a course, we would be no better than a hoard of lemmings who blindly follow a deluded leader.

Belief in the bodily resurrection of Jesus Christ is essential to saving faith.

—John Lody.

SCRIPTURE LESSON TEXT

LUKE 24:36 And as they thus spake, Jesus himself stood in the midst of them, and saith unto them, Peace *be* unto you.

37 But they were terrified and affrighted, and supposed that they had seen a spirit.

38 And he said unto them, Why are ye troubled? and why do thoughts arise in your hearts?

39 Behold my hands and my feet, that it is I myself: handle me, and see; for a spirit hath not flesh and bones, as ye see me have.

40 And when he had thus spoken, he shewed them *his* hands and *his* feet.

41 And while they yet believed not for joy, and wondered, he said unto them, Have ye here any meat?

42 And they gave him a piece of a broiled fish, and of an honeycomb.

43 And he took *it,* and did eat before them.

44 And he said unto them, These *are* the words which I spake unto you, while I was yet with you, that all things must be fulfilled, which were written in the law of Moses, and *in* the prophets, and *in* the psalms, concerning me.

45 Then opened he their understanding, that they might understand the scriptures,

46 And said unto them, Thus it is written, and thus it behoved Christ to suffer, and to rise from the dead the third day:

47 And that repentance and remission of sins should be preached in his name among all nations, beginning at Jerusalem.

48 And ye are witnesses of these things.

49 And, behold, I send the promise of my Father upon you: but tarry ye in the city of Jerusalem, until ye be endued with power from on high.

50 And he led them out as far as to Bethany, and he lifted up his hands, and blessed them.

51 And it came to pass, while he blessed them, he was parted from them, and carried up into heaven.

52 And they worshipped him, and returned to Jerusalem with great joy:

53 And were continually in the temple, praising and blessing God. Amen.

NOTES

Proofs of the Resurrection

Lesson Text: Luke 24:36-53

Related Scriptures: Acts 1:1-4; I Corinthians 15:3-8; I John 1:1-4

TIME: A.D. 30   PLACE: Jerusalem

GOLDEN TEXT—"These are the words which I spake unto you, while I was yet with you, that all things must be fulfilled, which were written in the law of Moses, and in the prophets, and in the psalms, concerning me" (Luke 24:44).

Lesson Exposition

SKEPTICAL DISCIPLES—
Luke 24:36-43

Afraid (Luke 24:36-37). Earlier in this chapter, two disciples had an unusual encounter with Jesus on the Emmaus road. After the Lord had revealed Himself to them, "he vanished out of their sight" (vs. 31). Quickly returning to Jerusalem, the two reported this to the others, who were meeting behind locked doors "for fear of the Jews" (John 20:19). They no doubt worried that the fate that had befallen their Master might be meted out to them as well.

As this week's text begins, the two disciples were continuing to relate to the others the events that had occurred, particularly that they had recognized Christ in the breaking of bread (Luke 24:35). Just then, Jesus appeared in their midst. Since He did not enter through the door, it is apparent that His glorified body was not subject to the same limitations all of us experience in our earthly bodies.

With regard to our own resurrected bodies, we can assume that like the glorified, resurrected body of the Lord Jesus, our new bodies will not be subject to current limitations. While there

will be continuity with our previous body (I Cor. 15:35-54), there will also be discontinuity. The new body will be strong, spiritual, heavenly, and no longer subject to pain, disease, sorrow, or death (Rev. 21:4).

Greeting the disciples in a typical Jewish fashion, the Saviour said, "Peace be unto you" (Luke 24:36). They felt anything but peace, however; "they were terrified and affrighted" (vs. 37).

Keep in mind that this was still the very day Jesus had risen. They had not anticipated the events of the past few days, but this was not because the Lord had not given them ample warning. For whatever reason, the disciples were unable (or unwilling) to process the information Christ had given concerning both His death and His resurrection. Consequently, they thought they were seeing a ghost—a mistake they had made on another occasion (Mark 6:49).

Admonished (Luke 24:38-39). Knowing their thoughts, Christ asked them why they were troubled in mind and heart. Had they actually listened more carefully to the things the Lord had been telling them the previous six months, they would not have been so surprised when it came to pass.

Challenging the disciples to examine His hands and feet, Christ wanted them to be fully convinced that what they were seeing was real. He was no apparition, but a person with a real body of "flesh and bones" (vs. 39). As alluded to earlier, we can assume that our own resurrected bodies will be similar. There is one thing we can be sure of—the resurrection of Christ was literal, physical, and bodily.

Assured (Luke 24:40-41). Having challenged the disciples to examine His body, the Lord permitted them to make sure that the wounds in His hands and feet were real. If He had been just a spirit, such examination would have been impossible, for, as He said, "A spirit hath not flesh and bones, as ye see me have" (vs. 39).

Affirmation (Luke 24:42-43). To further affirm that a literal resurrection had occurred, Jesus asked the disciples for something to eat. Surely a ghost would neither need nor have the ability to eat earthly food. They responded by giving Him some fish and honey. Eating it in their presence gave further proof of His actual resurrection.

SCRIPTURES FULFILLED— Luke 24:44-47

Minds opened (Luke 24:44-45). The disciples had to be convinced of the resurrection through visible, tangible proof. But had they listened to Jesus more carefully, they would have known that these things had been foretold by Him in concert with the prophetic testimony of the Old Testament.

Most of us have probably been taught to divide the Old Testament into four sections: Law, History, Poetry, and Prophecy. However, this was not the way the Scriptures were divided in

Christ's time—or in a modern Hebrew Bible.

The Old Testament was divided into three sections in the Jewish Scriptures: Law, Prophets, and Writings. These three sections contain twenty-four books, which are the same as the thirty-nine books of our Old Testament. The difference has to do with the fact that a Hebrew Bible often combines books that are divided in our Old Testament. As an example, all twelve Minor Prophets (Hosea through Malachi) were written on one scroll and seen as one book.

In a Hebrew Bible, the Law contains the same first five books of the Pentateuch found in our Bibles. The Prophets include the prophetic books (minus Daniel) and a number of historical books. The Writings begin with Psalms and include a variety of books, some coming from later biblical history.

When Christ said that the Law, Prophets, and Psalms were fulfilled in Him, He was declaring that everything in the Scriptures was pointing to Him. From our perspective, this means that when we read the Old Testament, we can anticipate finding Jesus there. This will include prophecies, promises, types, and figures.

It is one thing to hear and read the Scriptures; it is quite another to understand them. Christ therefore opened the disciples' minds to comprehend the Scriptures—an absolute necessity for those who were going to carry this message to the ends of the earth (Acts 1:8).

On the one hand, the Bible can be understood by all, as anyone might understand any other written document. But to fully comprehend the message that is contained therein, divine illumination is necessary. This was seen on Pentecost when Peter preached the Word but the Spirit convicted hearts (Acts 2:37).

Mission outlined (Luke 24:46-47). Reinforcing what He had already said, the Lord Jesus emphasized that the Scriptures foretold both His sacrificial death and His resurrection on the third day.

People may sometimes get the impression that Christ's death and resurrection automatically provides forgiveness for humanity. This, of course, is not true. Only as people turn from sin and turn to God—that is, truly repent—can they expect to be pardoned from sin. To be sure, repentance does not earn salvation; rather, repentance is a gracious work of God in the heart.

SPIRIT PROMISED—Luke 24:48-49

While all of us are to bear witness to the truth of the Bible and even present our personal testimonies of what the Lord has done for us, we are not witnesses in the sense that the original apostles were. They could give eyewitness testimony concerning both the miracles and the teachings of Christ. Seeing the risen Lord and being able to examine His wounds put them in a unique category of believers.

The disciples needed spiritual power to carry out their mission, so the Saviour urged them to stay in Jerusalem and wait for the coming of the Spirit (Acts 2:1-4). On the night before the crucifixion, Christ had given His disciples necessary teaching concerning the coming Holy Spirit (John 14—16), though at the time they most likely failed to comprehend it. With the arrival of the Spirit, however, they would be guided into all truth (14:26; 15:26; 16:13).

SAVIOUR ASCENDS—
Luke 24:50-53

Final blessing (Luke 24:50-51). If we had only Luke's Gospel, we might get the impression that Jesus ascended to heaven immediately after the resurrection. The other Gospels detail additional appearances of Christ, even in Galilee (Matt. 28:7; John 21:1-14). And Acts informs us that Christ was "seen of them forty days" (1:3). This probably means He appeared intermittently over a forty-day period, after which He ascended (vss. 9-11).

Followers' return (Luke 24:52-53). That the disciples "worshipped him" indicates that they were now fully convinced of Jesus' identity. Hence, we can understand why they had "great joy" as they returned to the city to await the coming of the Spirit.

Naturally, they worshipped in the temple, the Jewish place of worship. Luke's Gospel begins in the temple, and it concludes in the same place.
—*John Alva Owston.*

QUESTIONS

1. What do we know about Christ's body after His resurrection?
2. Why did the disciples think they had seen a spirit?
3. What things did Jesus do to convince His followers that they were not just seeing a ghost?
4. What is meant by the Law, Prophets, and Psalms?
5. How is the Hebrew Bible both like and unlike our Old Testament?
6. Why was it important that the minds of the disciples be opened to understand the Scriptures?
7. What is repentance? Why is it necessary for us to repent?
8. What were the apostles to wait for in Jerusalem?
9. How long did Christ make appearances to His disciples?
10. What was one thing the disciples did while waiting in Jerusalem?
—*John Alva Owston.*

PRACTICAL POINTS

1. If we think all our doubts would be resolved if we could just see Jesus, look at the Eleven (Luke 24:36-38)!

2. Jesus shows incomparable patience in overcoming our doubts (vss. 39-43).

3. When we get rattled by the seemingly unexpected, Jesus carefully reminds us of our mission (vss. 44-48).

4. The promise of the Father comes to those who obediently wait for it in faith (vs. 49).

5. Although Jesus is not physically with us now, we are continually surrounded by His presence and joy (vss. 50-53).

—Kenneth A. Sponsler.

RESEARCH AND DISCUSSION

1. How does the fact that the disciples thought they were seeing a ghost attest to the reality of the resurrection (Luke 24:37)? How might conspirators have written this account?

2. Was the risen Jesus actually hungry when He asked for food (vs. 41)? What was His likely purpose in making the request?

3. Since Jesus' explanation of the Scriptures was not recorded for us, how can we be enlightened as the Eleven were (vss. 44-45)?

4. How well have we been doing in the preaching of repentance and remission from sin in Jesus' name throughout the world (vs. 47)?

5. How was Jesus' ascension—a departure from His people—in reality a great blessing for them (vss. 51-53)?

—Kenneth A. Sponsler.

Golden Text Illuminated

"These are the words which I spake unto you, while I was yet with you, that all things must be fulfilled, which were written in the law of Moses, and in the prophets, and in the psalms, concerning me" (Luke 24:44).

Jesus fulfilled all of God's promises, and in the lives of believers He is always faithful to do what He promised to do. However, we sometimes make claims on His promises that we do not have a right to make. Three questions help us understand the issues involved in claiming God's promises.

1. Is it a promise for me?
2. Are there any conditional parts to the promise?
3. Do I understand there may be a difference between God's timing and my own?

Humans are constrained by time; God is not. That is why the apostle Peter wrote that a thousand years is as a day and a day is as a thousand years in God's sight (II Pet. 3:8).

God has an unchangeable plan, and He works out "all things after the counsel of his own will" (Eph. 1:11). He needs no one's advice. Each event in His plan will happen at His appointed time. We must not conclude that God is unfaithful simply because He does not fulfill His promise at the time we would prefer. His timing is perfect.

The old saying is true: You cannot break God's promises by leaning on them. He will always fulfill His promises. It is essential, however, that we have a biblical understanding of these promises.

—Joseph E. Falkner.

Scripture Lesson Text

JOHN 6:22 The day following, when the people which stood on the other side of the sea saw that there was none other boat there, save that one whereinto his disciples were entered, and that Jesus went not with his disciples into the boat, but *that* his disciples were gone away alone;

23 (Howbeit there came other boats from Tiberias nigh unto the place where they did eat bread, after that the Lord had given thanks:)

24 When the people therefore saw that Jesus was not there, neither his disciples, they also took shipping, and came to Capernaum, seeking for Jesus.

25 And when they had found him on the other side of the sea, they said unto him, Rabbi, when camest thou hither?

26 Jesus answered them and said, Verily, verily, I say unto you, Ye seek me, not because ye saw the miracles, but because ye did eat of the loaves, and were filled.

27 Labour not for the meat which perisheth, but for that meat which endureth unto everlasting life, which the Son of man shall give unto you: for him hath God the Father sealed.

28 Then said they unto him, What shall we do, that we might work the works of God?

29 Jesus answered and said unto them, This is the work of God, that ye believe on him whom he hath sent.

30 They said therefore unto him, What sign shewest thou then, that we may see, and believe thee? what dost thou work?

31 Our fathers did eat manna in the desert; as it is written, He gave them bread from heaven to eat.

32 Then Jesus said unto them, Verily, verily, I say unto you, Moses gave you not that bread from heaven; but my Father giveth you the true bread from heaven.

33 For the bread of God is he which cometh down from heaven, and giveth life unto the world.

34 Then said they unto him, Lord, evermore give us this bread.

35 And Jesus said unto them, I am the bread of life: he that cometh to me shall never hunger; and he that believeth on me shall never thirst.

NOTES

The Bread of Life

Lesson Text: John 6:22-35

Related Scriptures: Exodus 16:4-18; Isaiah 55:1-7; John 6:1-13

TIME: A.D. 29   PLACE: Sea of Galilee

GOLDEN TEXT—"Jesus said unto them, I am the bread of life: he that cometh to me shall never hunger; and he that believeth on me shall never thirst" (John 6:35).

Lesson Exposition

WHERE IS JESUS?—John 6:22-27

Missing Jesus (John 6:22-23). At the beginning of chapter 6 we read of Jesus feeding the multitude near the city of Bethsaida. Toward evening His disciples boarded a boat and set out across the sea toward Capernaum (vs. 17). Jesus joined them later by walking to them on the water (vss. 18-21). The next day the people started to search for Him around Bethsaida, knowing that He had not sailed with His disciples when they left.

It soon became a source of confusion to them, for they had seen the disciples get into the one small boat and leave and had seen Jesus remain behind. In fact, they had probably seen Him leave their midst and head for the mountain, where He went to pray. They expected to find Him the next morning.

One of the things that always concerned Jesus was the propensity of the people to hope He had come to be the one who would deliver them from the dominion of Rome. Their concept of the coming Messiah was much more political than spiritual,

Seeking Jesus (John 6:24-25). We are not told why boats came from Tiberias, but we wonder whether word of the miracle of the feeding of the crowd had spread that far and others were now coming to see Jesus too. When the people looking for Jesus at Bethsaida could not find Him anywhere, they got into these boats and headed for Capernaum, "seeking for Jesus." He had made such a huge impact on them by feeding the crowd that they were determined to see more of Him.

Sure enough, Jesus was there! Upon finding Him, the people had just one question. When did He get there?

Hearing Jesus (John 6:26-27). Jesus knew their hearts. He knew they were seeking Him in order to see what other physical benefit He would provide them.

Jesus told them they needed to be looking for spiritual food instead.

He explained that spiritual nourishment, as opposed to physical, will endure forever.

WHAT SHALL WE DO?— John 6:28-31

Asking what to do (John 6:28-29). Apparently the listeners thought Jesus meant there were certain things they needed to do in order to have such spiritual nourishment. They had the

40

idea that they would gain salvation by earning it. If they could just prove themselves worthy of being accepted by God, they would be all right.

Jesus responded by telling them the only work expected of them was to believe in Him. This is not work in the sense we usually think but rather a matter of responding to God's offer of salvation through His Son. There is no activity that can merit salvation and eternal life.

Asking for a sign (John 6:30-31). These Jews evidently understood that Jesus was claiming to be the Messiah, so they asked for a messianic proof of some kind. The irony is that they had just seen Him miraculously multiply five loaves of bread and two small fish in order to feed thousands of people! How could they not see that a sign had already been given? Why ask for something else?

These people were attempting to minimize what Jesus had done by comparing it with what Moses had done in the wilderness. Moses, they said, had provided manna for a huge entourage of Israelites for the bulk of forty years. Jesus had merely fed several thousand once. If He really was the Messiah, surely He could do better than that!

The people might also have been comparing the fact that Moses had provided bread from heaven, while all Jesus did was give them earthly loaves.

MAY WE HAVE THIS BREAD?—
John 6:32-35

The Bread of God (John 6:32-33). Jesus quickly informed them that they were thinking incorrectly; it was God, not Moses, who had sent the bread, or manna, from heaven. When the manna was first provided, Moses pointed out that it had come from God. The contrast Jesus made was between the bread that came from heaven during Moses' day and "the true bread" that was now available to them. The big-gest difference is that the bread sent during Moses' day satisfied physical needs only; the "true bread," however, would satisfy spiritually and eternally.

Jesus then said plainly, "The bread of God is he which cometh down from heaven"—Jesus Himself (vs. 33).

The Bread of Life (John 6:34-35). It is obvious from this request from the Jews that they did not comprehend what Jesus was saying about Himself. They asked Him to give them this bread and to keep giving it to them.

Jesus finally had to make clear statements for them, and He began by identifying Himself as the Bread of Life. These people needed to know that He was not referring to physical bread but to the spiritual sustenance He could give them if they received Him into their lives.

—Keith E. Eggert.

QUESTIONS

1. What was confusing to the people the morning after the disciples had left Bethsaida by boat?
2. What misguided ideas did Jesus continually encounter?
3. What enabled the people to go to Capernaum to seek Jesus?
4. What did Jesus say was the real reason the people were seeking Him?
5. What kind of food did Jesus tell them they should be looking for?
6. What did the people misunderstand about salvation?
7. How did Jesus describe the work they should do?
8. Why did they ask for a sign?
9. What did Jesus say about the bread that they said Moses gave?
10. Who is the real Bread of Life, and what does He provide?

—Keith E. Eggert.

PRACTICAL POINTS

1. Fallen humans are prone to seek material rather than spiritual satisfaction (John 6:22-26).
2. If we come to Jesus for any other reason than to worship Him as Lord and Saviour, we are at enmity with God's plan (vs. 27).
3. Believing the gospel seems too simple and trivial to the unbelieving heart (vss. 28-31).
4. Unbelievers give glory to men rather than God (vs. 32).
5. Jesus Himself provides all we need to sustain the abundant Christian life (vs. 33).
6. Unbelievers hear the living words of Jesus Christ but are without understanding (vss. 34-35).

— *John Lody.*

RESEARCH AND DISCUSSION

1. Research and discuss the priority of the spiritual realm over the material realm in the Christian life. How is such a priority to be lived out on a daily basis?
2. What are the proper motives for making a profession of faith? Is a profession that is caused by wrong motives always false?
3. If believing the gospel is such a simple act, why do so many resist the call to believe? What are current religious ideas that can tend to complicate salvation with human additions?
4. How did Jesus speak to crowds? Contrast His intended meanings with the crowd's understanding of Him (or lack thereof).

— *John Lody.*

Golden Text Illuminated

"And Jesus said unto them, I am the Bread of Life: he that cometh to me shall never hunger; and he that believeth on me shall never thirst" (John 6:35).

Our golden text for this week happens to be the final verse of our lesson text. Of obvious relevance to this week's text is Jesus' feeding of the multitude (John 6:1-14).

The crowd that now followed Jesus around the shore to Capernaum (vs. 24) came because they expected Him to give them all another free meal. When they finally found Him, they asked a question that sounded innocent enough, "Rabbi, when camest thou hither?" (vs. 25). But Jesus, knowing their true intentions, rebuked them for their unbelief in spite of witnessing such a great miracle. He exhorted them to work for food that gives eternal life rather than for food that perishes with the physical body.

As their dialogue with Jesus continued, the crowd's thinking remained fixed on earthly things, so their misunderstanding of Jesus escalated. At one point, they actually had the audacity to demand another miracle from Him before they would believe what He was saying (cf. vs. 30)! They wanted Him to rain manna down on them as Moses had done.

It was at this lowest point of spirituality for His audience that Jesus revealed to them that He Himself was the Bread of Life that they so desperately needed. The person who puts trust in Jesus will never lack for spiritual nourishment, for He is the never-ending source of heavenly food, the very Word of God.

— *John Lody.*

SCRIPTURE LESSON TEXT

JOHN 8:12 Then spake Jesus again unto them, saying, I am the light of the world: he that followeth me shall not walk in darkness, but shall have the light of life.

13 The Pharisees therefore said unto him, Thou bearest record of thyself; thy record is not true.

14 Jesus answered and said unto them, Though I bear record of myself, *yet* my record is true: for I know whence I came, and whither I go; but ye cannot tell whence I come, and whither I go.

15 Ye judge after the flesh; I judge no man.

16 And yet if I judge, my judgment is true: for I am not alone, but I and the Father that sent me.

17 It is also written in your law, that the testimony of two men is true.

18 I am one that bear witness of myself, and the Father that sent me beareth witness of me.

19 Then said they unto him, Where is thy Father? Jesus answered, Ye neither know me, nor my Father: if ye had known me, ye should have known my Father also.

20 These words spake Jesus in the treasury, as he taught in the temple: and no man laid hands on him; for his hour was not yet come.

12:44 Jesus cried and said, He that believeth on me, believeth not on me, but on him that sent me.

45 And he that seeth me seeth him that sent me.

46 I am come a light into the world, that whosoever believeth on me should not abide in darkness.

NOTES

The Light of the World

Lesson Text: John 8:12-20; 12:44-46

Related Scriptures: Isaiah 9:2-6; Matthew 5:14-16;
John 1:1-10; I John 5:5-13

TIMES: A.D. 29; 30   PLACE: Jerusalem

GOLDEN TEXT—"I am the light of the world: he that followeth me shall not walk in darkness, but shall have the light of life" (John 8:12).

Lesson Exposition

THE OFFER OF LIGHT—
John 8:12-16

Jesus' claim (John 8:12). We live in a world under Satan's sway (John 14:30; II Cor. 4:4; Eph. 2:2), though it is under the ultimate control of God. Evil is prevalent everywhere on this globe.

There is only one hope for dispelling this darkness; it is found in the Person of Jesus Christ, the Son of God. He boldly declared, "I am the light of the world: he that followeth me shall not walk in darkness, but shall have the light of life" (John 8:12).

It is likely that Jesus was still at the Feast of Tabernacles (7:2). During this feast, large lamps were lit, and the people held festive dances of celebration. Jesus used this ritual to declare Himself to be the light of the entire world, not just the local area. Jesus exposes sin and dispels darkness.

Jesus' knowledge (John 8:13-14). As usual, the Pharisees challenged Jesus immediately, this time with the accusation that all He had for validating His statement was a false self-witness.

Jesus' response was that He could bear witness to Himself because His words were always the truth. He was

not a liar, as they assumed. In addition, He knew where He had come from and where He was going. They knew nothing about this. While this might not have sounded like very good evidence to His critics, we understand that He was challenging them with facts that they should have known about their Messiah but did not.

Jesus' judgment (John 8:15-16). Jesus said the Pharisees judged according to the flesh, that is, by what they could see and hear only. They looked at external things and judged by human standards, with no concept of how God views things.

Jesus said that He would not judge the way they did ("I judge no man") but that when the time came for Him to judge, His judgment would be true.

THE OFFER OF WITNESSES—
John 8:17-20

Bearing testimony (John 8:17-18). The Mosaic law stated, "At the mouth of two witnesses, or three witnesses, shall he that is worthy of death be put to death; but at the mouth of one witness he shall not be put to death" (Deut. 17:6).

The Pharisees tried to apply this principle to Jesus. So now Jesus proceeded to point out that the law did require two witnesses for validating truth and that He did indeed have two witnesses. He bore witness regarding Himself, and the Father who sent Him also testified for Him.

John's Gospel has already established the fact that John the Baptist had come as a witness for Jesus (John 1:7; 5:33). The Samaritan woman had said, "Come, see a man, which told me all things that ever I did: is not this the Christ?" (4:29).

There had already been plenty of proof regarding Jesus, but the Pharisees refused to acknowledge it.

Knowing God (John 8:19-20). If Jesus was going to claim His Father as His witness, the Pharisees wanted to know where he was. They were thinking, as usual, in human terms only; so they asked about His earthly father. Since they had rejected Jesus' message and claims of deity, they could not understand how God could be Jesus' Father. Jesus replied that the question itself revealed their ignorance. They did not know Him or His Father. If they had known Him, they would have known His Father too.

It is quite possible that there were people present who were eager to arrest Jesus and get rid of Him. John explained that even though this was the case, no one laid hands on Him, simply because "his hour was not yet come." The implication is that they were ready to act but were divinely restrained from doing so.

THE OFFER OF ESCAPE FROM DARKNESS—John 12:44-46

Believing in God (John 12:44-45). Jesus assured the people that anyone who believed in Him was at the same time believing in God, His Father.

Living in light (John 12:46). Once again Jesus made His claim: He came as a light into the world, and whoever believes in Him will not walk in darkness. It is a matter of having spiritual understanding as opposed to being ignorant of God's ways.

It is sometimes difficult for unbelievers to comprehend the reality of their lack of spiritual understanding. Many think they have insight into spirituality, but their knowledge is false. That is why it is important to emphasize the most important matter first: believe in the Lord Jesus Christ in order to be saved.

—Keith E. Eggert.

QUESTIONS

1. Why is there so much darkness in the world, and what is our hope?
2. Why did the Pharisees challenge Jesus' self-witness?
3. Why did Jesus speak of where He came from and where He was going?
4. How did Jesus say His judgment would differ from that of the Pharisees?
5. What Old Testament basis of testimony did the Pharisees use against Jesus?
6. How did Jesus respond?
7. What did Jesus mean when He said that they knew neither Him nor His Father?
8. Why was no one able to apprehend Jesus?
9. What did Jesus mean when He said that whoever believes in Him would not walk in darkness?
10. What must happen before people can understand true spirituality?

—Keith E. Eggert.

PRACTICAL POINTS

1. When we have adequate light, whether we are speaking of physical light or spiritual light, we neither stumble nor fall (John 8:12).
2. We should readily accept the truth whenever we find it (vss. 13-14).
3. If we agree with God, we will not misjudge anything (vss. 15-18).
4. Many questions arise simply because we are not fully following God (vs. 19).
5. If we are in God's hands and following His will, we need not fear what people might do to us (vs. 20).
6. We cannot know God except through Jesus, and we cannot come to God except through Jesus (12:44-46).

—Ralph Woodworth.

RESEARCH AND DISCUSSION

1. Are we the light of the world in the same way that Jesus is (John 8:12; cf. Matt. 5:14)?
2. Why did most of the Pharisees find it so difficult to accept Jesus as the Son of God (John 8:13; cf. Luke 7:30)?
3. Earlier, Jesus had said that the Father gave Him authority to judge. Why did He say here that He judges no one (John 8:15; cf. 5:27; Acts 10:42; II Tim. 4:1)?
4. How can we be sure a witness is telling the truth (John 8:13-17; cf. 15:27; Acts 22:14-15)?
5. Do you think God has a timetable for all things, including your life (John 8:20; cf. Eccl. 3:1)?

—Ralph Woodworth.

Golden Text Illuminated

"I am the light of the world: he that followeth me shall not walk in darkness, but shall have the light of life" (John 8:12).

Our golden text is only one of a number of verses in the Bible, and especially in John's Gospel, to teach that the light we really need is available only from God, who is light Himself (John 1:4; I John 1:5). We need God's light because this world is in moral darkness. God has already given physical light, and He stands ready to give moral and ethical light to the one who recognizes the need and reaches out by faith to the Lord.

God is Light; the Lord Jesus is Light; and the Word of God is Light also (Ps. 119:105). In addition, the Holy Spirit's ministry, in part, is shining light into the dark corners of the heart to expose sin so that we can be convicted and confess it to God. The Spirit also enlightens those who read His Word (cf. I Cor. 2:14).

In our golden text, Jesus goes on to state that those who follow Him will not walk in darkness. He does not mean He will provide a physical light on a dark night. Rather, a disciple of Christ will be given the wisdom he needs to make day-to-day decisions. We have to want spiritual light to receive it, and the promise is that those who are genuine followers of the Lord will understand His Word and be able to apply it to everyday decisions.

The believer should not plead ignorance about right and wrong, especially if he has the Bible and is serious about hiding it in his heart.

—Darrell W. McKay.

SCRIPTURE LESSON TEXT

JOHN 10:7 Then said Jesus unto them again, Verily, verily, I say unto you, I am the door of the sheep.

8 All that ever came before me are thieves and robbers: but the sheep did not hear them.

9 I am the door: by me if any man enter in, he shall be saved, and shall go in and out, and find pasture.

10 The thief cometh not, but for to steal, and to kill, and to destroy: I am come that they might have life, and that they might have *it* more abundantly.

11 I am the good shepherd: the good shepherd giveth his life for the sheep.

12 But he that is an hireling, and not the shepherd, whose own the sheep are not, seeth the wolf coming, and leaveth the sheep, and fleeth: and the wolf catcheth them, and scattereth the sheep.

13 The hireling fleeth, because he is an hireling, and careth not for the sheep.

14 I am the good shepherd, and know my *sheep,* and am known of mine.

15 As the Father knoweth me, even so know I the Father: and I lay down my life for the sheep.

16 And other sheep I have, which are not of this fold: them also I must bring, and they shall hear my voice; and there shall be one fold, *and* one shepherd.

17 Therefore doth my Father love me, because I lay down my life, that I might take it again.

18 No man taketh it from me, but I lay it down of myself. I have power to lay it down, and I have power to take it again. This commandment have I received of my Father.

NOTES

The Good Shepherd

Lesson Text: John 10:7-18

Related Scriptures: Psalm 23:1-6; Jeremiah 23:1-6;
Ezekiel 34:10-25; I Peter 5:1-4

TIME: A.D. 29   PLACE: Jerusalem

GOLDEN TEXT—"I am the good shepherd: the good shepherd giveth his life for the sheep" (John 10:11).

Lesson Exposition

THE ONLY DOOR—John 10:7-10

Ignoring the thieves and robbers (John 10:7-8). Jesus talked about a shepherd entering the sheepfold to call out his own sheep by name. It was common for more than one flock to be kept in the same fold overnight, but the flocks could be easily separated because the sheep knew their own master's voice. The shepherd always used the door of the fold for getting his sheep, so anyone trying to get to them by some other way would immediately be exposed as an impostor.

Jesus referred to Himself as the Door for the sheep. It was common for a shepherd to get his sheep inside the fold and then lie down across the opening so he became a barrier against any wild animals or thieves. Jesus is a protector for His sheep. A door is a means of entry. Jesus is the means of entry into the family of God.

Jesus repeated the thought found in John 10:1 about thieves and robbers trying to get to the sheep (vs. 8). This is a reference to the Jewish leaders who were leading the people astray.

Entering the door to good pasture (John 10:9-10). When the shepherd took his sheep through the door into the fold, he was putting them in a place of safety and security, where enemies and wild animals could not get them. In this way they were safe, saved from the dangers outside the fold. Jesus' reference to being saved refers to spiritual salvation, where there is safety from Satan and eternal destruction. Furthermore, we are spiritually nourished from then on, as indicated by our finding pasture (vs. 9).

Jesus then made another reference to false teachers, or thieves, who rob people of truth. All they can do is steal, kill, and destroy. In taking away the truth, they lead people toward an eternity apart from God. Jesus, on the other hand, came to give people eternal life and a present life that is fulfilling.

**THE ONLY SHEPHERD—
John 10:11-15**

Self-sacrifice (John 10:11). Every shepherd faced certain dangers in his occupation. Robbers might appear. Wild animals were always lurking. Good shepherds were willing to lay their lives on the line to protect their sheep. Jesus was certainly willing to do that for His "sheep." The false teachers referred to earlier would never be willing to make such a sacrifice for their followers.

Self-preservation (John 10:12-13). When it comes to assisting a shepherd, a hireling has no ownership of the flock; so he would never even consider giving his life for the sheep under his care. When he sees the wolf coming to attack, he will run in order to protect himself. This leaves the sheep unprotected, and the wolf runs in among them, killing some of them and scattering the rest. In contrast, the Good Shepherd owns, cares, feeds, protects, and dies for His sheep.

Selflessness (John 10:14-15). We noted earlier that sheep know the voice of their shepherd. He also knows each of his sheep, because as their owner he loves them and cares about them. Jesus assured His listeners that as the Good Shepherd, He knows each of His sheep and they know Him. What an encouragement! He knows us, and as we learn about Him, we can grow to know Him more deeply.

The example Jesus gave to illustrate this closeness was His relationship with His Father. They know each other deeply and have for all eternity past! This is what made Jesus willing to lay down His life for the sheep.

THE WHOLE FLOCK—
John 10:16-18

Other sheep (John 10:16). The "other sheep" who are "not of this fold" is a reference to the Gentiles, many of whom in succeeding years would come to know Jesus as their Shepherd. Jesus offered salvation to the Jews first, but His intention was to expand that offer to Gentiles as well. This would result in a single flock under the one true Shepherd. Believers are united in Christ and no longer separated.

Resurrection power (John 10:17-18). For the third and fourth times Jesus said in these verses He was laying down His life for the sheep (cf. vss. 11, 15). But He added an important note here—namely, that He was doing this voluntarily. Because of Jesus' obedience unto death, the Father has a special love for Him. He laid it down by His own choice because this was His Father's plan.

Jesus claimed ultimate authority when He said He had the power to take His own life back again after having laid it down in death. We see His deity here, for only God can give life and have the authority Jesus claimed here. He is God, just as His Father is God.

—Keith E. Eggert.

QUESTIONS

1. What factor made it possible for a shepherd to always lead his own sheep out every morning?

2. What did Jesus mean when He referred to Himself as the Door (John 10:7)?

3. Who were the "thieves" (vs. 8) of Jesus' day, and what were they doing to harm the people?

4. How does the sheepfold picture our salvation?

5. What was the difference between a shepherd and a hireling?

6. What do we know about Jesus as our personal Shepherd?

7. How did Jesus illustrate the relationship He has with His sheep?

8. Who are the "other sheep" (vs. 16)?

9. What important truth did Jesus communicate about His death?

10. What did Jesus do that no one else can ever do after death?

—Keith E. Eggert.

PRACTICAL POINTS

1. The Holy Spirit is our source of discernment as to whether a voice belongs to Jesus (John 10:7-8).
2. Those who come to the Father through Jesus have ready access to all God's goodness (vs. 9).
3. Beware! Satan continually tries to sneak into the church to ruin it in any way he can (vs. 10).
4. In contrast to everyone else, only Jesus is willing to give all for His elect (vs. 11).
5. Hired workers will quit when the work costs them more than they value the pay (vss. 12-13).
6. Those who truly belong to Jesus will instinctively respond only to His leading (vss. 14-18).

—*John Lody.*

RESEARCH AND DISCUSSION

1. What does it mean to have spiritual discernment? How is it acquired? How is it developed?
2. Satan is our greatest enemy. Has he been prowling around your church?
3. How committed are you to the welfare of God's people? Could anything cause you to forsake your present church? What about the church in general? Meditate on the depth of your commitment.
4. If Christians have the mind of Christ (I Cor. 2:16) and the discernment of the indwelling Holy Spirit (I John 2:20, 27), why do so many Christians get confused about God's will for their lives and fall prey to false teachers (cf. vss. 19, 26)?

—*John Lody.*

Golden Text Illuminated

"I am the good shepherd: the good shepherd giveth his life for the sheep" (John 10:11).

Our golden text for this week is taken from the last of the seven discourses of Jesus in John's Gospel: the "Good Shepherd" discourse. He is the Good Shepherd who gives His life for the sheep. Jesus was contrasting Himself with false messiahs who had been misleading God's people (cf. Acts 5:34-37). All their ministries had come to naught, and their followers had been scattered.

Besides our lesson text for this week, Psalm 23 is famous for giving us an accurate description of the Lord as our Good Shepherd. The Lord always leads His flock into situations where they will find abundant sustenance and resources to grow (vs. 2). He restores His people's lost souls, keeping them on righteous paths (vs. 3).

Even during the darkest times of their lives, the sheep need never succumb to fear, for the Lord is present with them to protect them and see them safely home. He is their hope and courage in the face of all opposition (vs. 4). Even in the face of great danger from their enemies, He abundantly provides for them (vs. 5).

The Lord's love and goodness surrounds His people throughout all the days of their lives, and afterward He welcomes them into eternal pastures where they will forever graze safely under His eternally watchful eyes (vs. 6).

As our Good Shepherd, Christ knows each and every person with all the profound knowledge and covenant love of our Creator and Saviour.

—*John Lody.*

SCRIPTURE LESSON TEXT

JOHN 11:17 Then when Jesus came, he found that he had *lain* in the grave four days already.

18 Now Bethany was nigh unto Jerusalem, about fifteen furlongs off:

19 And many of the Jews came to Martha and Mary, to comfort them concerning their brother.

20 Then Martha, as soon as she heard that Jesus was coming, went and met him: but Mary sat *still* in the house.

21 Then said Martha unto Jesus, Lord, if thou hadst been here, my brother had not died.

22 But I know, that even now, whatsoever thou wilt ask of God, God will give *it* thee.

23 Jesus saith unto her, Thy brother shall rise again.

24 Martha saith unto him, I know that he shall rise again in the resurrection at the last day.

25 Jesus said unto her, I am the resurrection, and the life: he that believeth in me, though he were dead, yet shall he live:

26 And whosoever liveth and believeth in me shall never die. Believest thou this?

27 She saith unto him, Yea, Lord: I believe that thou art the Christ, the Son of God, which should come into the world.

NOTES

The Resurrection and the Life

Lesson Text: John 11:17-27

Related Scriptures: Daniel 12:1-3; John 11:1-16, 28-45;
I Corinthians 15:20-26; Philippians 3:7-14

TIME: A.D. 30　　　　　　　　　　　　　　　PLACE: Bethany

GOLDEN TEXT—"I am the resurrection, and the life: he that believeth in me, though he were dead, yet shall he live" (John 11:25).

Lesson Exposition

THE TOMB—John 11:17-19

Death and burial (John 11:17). By the time Jesus arrived in Bethany, Lazarus had already been in his tomb four days. Since it would have taken at least one day to travel there after He waited two extra days before leaving, Lazarus probably was dead by the time Jesus received word of his illness. Since He is omniscient, He knew all about what was happening and what He was going to do about it; so He sensed no need to hurry. This was going to give Him an opportunity to reveal Himself in His divine glory.

It seems that Jesus' primary purpose in not heading immediately to Bethany was for the sake of His disciples. From the concern they expressed and the comments they made, it seems quite certain that they had more to learn before they would be ready to assume their ministries after Jesus was gone.

Comforting friends (John 11:18-19). The mention of "many of the Jews" indicates there were people there from Jerusalem as well as Bethany.

The close location explains why many friends had traveled there to comfort Lazarus's sisters, Mary and Martha. Such a large number of friends also indicates that this was a rather prominent family in the town.

It was customary for the Jewish people to have lengthy times of mourning following a death, often at least a week. By the time Jesus and His disciples arrived, the mourning had begun. Many people were there to comfort Mary and Martha.

THE HOPE—John 11:20-23

A disappointment (John 11:20-21). As soon as Martha heard that Jesus was coming, she left the house to go meet Him. Mary stayed behind and sat in the house.

Martha's first words to Jesus were an expression of regret. She probably knew that Lazarus was dead before Jesus received word of his illness, so this was not a complaint against Him. It was, rather, an expression of confidence. She knew that if Jesus had been there, Lazarus would not have died. Jesus had been known to heal others, so she was confident He also would have healed her brother.

A promise (John 11:22-23). Jesus assured Martha that her brother would rise again. How different it is for those of us who believe in resurrection than for those who believe death ends everything! Death is separation. Physical death is the separation of the immaterial part of us from the material. Spiritual death is being separated from God and having no relationship with Him. Eternal death is permanent separation from the presence of God and an eternity spent in hell instead.

THE REASSURANCE—John 11:24-27

Resurrection promised (John 11:24-25). Jesus' statement to Martha did not provide her with any immediate comfort, for she was thinking of resurrection the way the Old Testament refers to it. She was no more made hopeful by Jesus' presence than she had been in His absence. Martha was thinking only in terms of the end times, not of something immediate.

Jesus then made an "I am" statement. He stated that He is the Resurrection and the Life. He could confidently say that even if those who believe in Him die, they will live again. Physical death may come, but eternal death never will.

Eternal life promised (John 11:26-27). It would be very difficult for those outside of God's family to understand what Jesus meant when He said, "Whosoever liveth and believeth in me shall never die." Reality reveals to us that everyone who lives on earth dies, without any exceptions. That includes believers as well as unbelievers. So what did Jesus mean?

Once we have become part of God's family through faith in Jesus Christ as our personal Saviour, we will never lose that family relationship. From that moment on, we possess eternal life (cf. John 3:16; 5:24; 10:28). Jesus said this: "And I give unto them eternal life; and they shall never perish, neither shall any man pluck them out of my hand. My Father, which gave me them, is greater than all; and no man is able to pluck them out of my Father's hand" (10:28-29).

Jesus wanted to know whether Martha believed this. Her response was that she did. She revealed a deep, genuine faith in Him when she called Him the Christ and the Son of God who was to come into the world. She understood that He was the promised Messiah and that everything was going to be all right with Him in control. Her faith was vindicated when Jesus miraculously raised Lazarus from the dead.

—*Keith E. Eggert.*

QUESTIONS

1. How long had Lazarus been buried when Jesus got to Bethany, and when had he probably died?
2. Why did Jesus delay His return to Bethany?
3. Why were there so many people at the home, and what does this indicate?
4. Which sister went to Jesus right away, and what did she say?
5. What did Jesus promise Martha?
6. What kinds of death are referred to in Scripture?
7. What "I am" statement did Jesus make at this time, and what was He claiming by it?
8. What did Jesus say about believers dying physically?
9. What did Jesus mean by saying that believers will never die?
10. How did Martha respond to Jesus' question about whether she believed what He said?

—*Keith E. Eggert.*

PRACTICAL POINTS

1. Even in our deaths we can fulfill God's sovereign plan and glorify Him (John 11:17-18).
2. Only Christians have a true hope that comforts and consoles those who mourn (vs. 19).
3. Christians vary in their reactions to the death of a loved one (vs. 20).
4. Jesus is with us, even when we think He is absent (vs. 21).
5. Faith that believes in the power of Christ to right all wrongs is never in vain (vss. 22-24).
6. True faith in Jesus Christ is never a mere mental or academic exercise; it is a matter of life and death (vss. 25-27)!

—John Lody.

RESEARCH AND DISCUSSION

1. Lazarus's death was allowed in order to bear witness to Jesus' power. How does this violate most people's expectation of what God is like?
2. How are Christians uniquely equipped to deal with the most profound tragedies of life?
3. Do all Christians react to death the same way? Should they, given the content of our faith?
4. During times when we feel God is far away from us, is He really? What does it mean to feel God's presence?
5. What is the relationship between doctrines of faith and the practices of daily Christian living? How does the fact of Christ's resurrection impact your daily life?

—John Lody.

Golden Text Illuminated

"I am the resurrection, and the life: he that believeth in me, though he were dead, yet shall he live" (John 11:25).

Where is Jesus when you need Him? Have you ever felt that way? He will never leave you or forsake you. That promise is still in Hebrews 13:6. So why do you feel so lonely?

Mary and Martha must have felt that way when Lazarus died. They were close friends with Jesus. He did not arrive until four days after Lazarus's death. He had delayed His trip to Bethany, where Lazarus lived with his sisters. It looked like pretty bad timing.

Understand this about God's timing, though. It is always perfect, but it does not always align with our schedules. God does not always show up when we think He must. Take a look at Habakkuk 2:3. If ever there were a verse that seemed to contradict itself, this is it. How do we explain the apparent conflict?

There is a difference between God's outlook on time and our own. He is an eternal Being, without beginning or end. Time does not affect Him. That is why He could tell Habakkuk that the fulfillment of the vision would not tarry.

There are two things we need to remember. First, we now live in a cursed world. Believers and unbelievers alike suffer the effects on our world.

Second, we have not yet experienced resurrection. We are not home yet, and we "groan, earnestly desiring to be clothed upon with our house which is from heaven" (II Cor. 5:2).

—Joseph E. Falkner.

SCRIPTURE LESSON TEXT

JOHN 15:1 I am the true vine, and my Father is the husbandman.

2 Every branch in me that beareth not fruit he taketh away: and every *branch* **that beareth fruit, he purgeth it, that it may bring forth more fruit.**

3 Now ye are clean through the word which I have spoken unto you.

4 Abide in me, and I in you. As the branch cannot bear fruit of itself, except it abide in the vine; no more can ye, except ye abide in me.

5 I am the vine, ye *are* the branches: He that abideth in me, and I in him, the same bringeth forth much fruit: for without me ye can do nothing.

6 If a man abide not in me, he is cast forth as a branch, and is withered; and men gather them, and cast them into the fire, and they are burned.

7 If ye abide in me, and my words abide in you, ye shall ask what ye will, and it shall be done unto you.

8 Herein is my Father glorified, that ye bear much fruit; so shall ye be my disciples.

9 As the Father hath loved me, so have I loved you: continue ye in my love.

10 If ye keep my commandments, ye shall abide in my love; even as I have kept my Father's commandments, and abide in his love.

11 These things have I spoken unto you, that my joy might remain in you, and *that* your joy might be full.

12 This is my commandment, That ye love one another, as I have loved you.

13 Greater love hath no man than this, that a man lay down his life for his friends.

14 Ye are my friends, if ye do whatsoever I command you.

15 Henceforth I call you not servants; for the servant knoweth not what his lord doeth: but I have called you friends; for all things that I have heard of my Father I have made known unto you.

16 Ye have not chosen me, but I have chosen you, and ordained you, that ye should go and bring forth fruit, and *that* **your fruit should remain: that whatsoever ye shall ask of the Father in my name, he may give it you.**

17 These things I command you, that ye love one another.

NOTES

The True Vine

Lesson Text: John 15:1-17

Related Scriptures: Isaiah 5:1-7; 27:2-6; Colossians 2:6-10; I John 2:24-29

TIME: A.D. 30   PLACE: Jerusalem

GOLDEN TEXT—"I am the vine, ye are the branches: He that abideth in me, and I in him, the same bringeth forth much fruit: for without me ye can do nothing" (John 15:5).

Lesson Exposition

**A COMMAND TO ABIDE—
John 15:1-8**

Bearing more fruit (John 15:1-2). Psalm 80:8-16 gives a clear analogy of Israel as God's vine. This psalm is a prayer for her restoration. Isaiah 5:1-7 describes Israel as a vineyard that was planted and nurtured by God, only to bring forth wild grapes. The lack of production by His vineyard caused God great disappointment.

With the proliferation of grapevines in Israel, the disciples could easily understand Jesus' message. He is the True Vine, producing for His Father what the nation had not. His Father is the farmer caring for his vineyard. Believers in Jesus are the branches He said are "in me" (John 15:2).

The farmer (God) takes special interest in the branches. Those that do not produce he "taketh away" (vs. 2). The Greek word here can mean "to lift," and since the branches are said to be in Christ, some Bible students believe the meaning is an encouraging one. It may picture the farmer seeing a branch hanging close to the ground, unable to produce and needing to be lifted up so that it can. Those already bearing fruit, however, are pruned so

that they will bear even more. It is clear that God works with His own in ways that make them more righteous.

Abiding in the Vine (John 15:3-4). "Pruning" refers to cutting a plant back in order to give the opportunity for new and fresh growth. The process God uses in pruning His children is at times very painful. It is through suffering and pain that we often grow the most and become more godly and productive.

Chastening for disobedience (John 15:5-6). There is a progression of thought in Jesus' words. He spoke first of no fruit, then of "fruit" and "more fruit" (vs. 2), and now of "much fruit" (vs. 5). Once again He clarified, "I am the vine, ye are the branches." It is only the person who abides in Him who will be able to bear "much fruit." The reason is that apart from Him, His followers can do nothing spiritually.

Verse 6 has been interpreted in a number of ways. Since the context is about branches in the vine, it seems to refer to those who do know the Lord. Perhaps the casting out speaks of a loss of fellowship, the withering to a loss of spiritual vitality, the vitality that is part of being in a right relationship with Christ, and the burning to the loss of reward at the time of judgment. Some think a better interpretation is to view this as referring to professing believers who are not truly saved and are judged accordingly.

Receiving what is requested (John 15:7-8). One of the most encouraging aspects of abiding in Christ is the reality of answered prayer. The person who abides in Christ knows the mind of Christ and as a result has a more effective prayer life. As others see our walk with Him and witness answered prayer, God is honored.

The concept of bearing fruit must include two ideas, one of which is the leading of others to saving faith in Jesus Christ. The other is found in Galatians 5:22-23. Jesus wants His followers to show others the way of salvation, but He also wants to see godliness displayed in their lives.

A COMMAND TO LOVE—
John 15:9-17

Abiding in Jesus' love (John 15:9-10). If we fully comprehended the love of which we speak, we would indeed abide in that love. The emphasis is on obedience to Jesus' commands. There is no mystical secret to abiding in the love of Jesus; it is simply a matter of listening to Him, learning what He wants us to be and do.

Loving as Jesus loves (John 15:11-13). Here is another blessing that is a result of abiding in Jesus: it yields the presence of joy in our lives.

The real test is now given: not only are we to respond by loving Jesus, but we are also to love one another in the same way Jesus loves us. Jesus set the standard as high as it could go by saying that there is no greater love possible than that which is shown when a person gives his life for his friends (vs. 13).

Learning from Jesus' love (John 15:14-15). Paul was a voluntary slave for Jesus, as we should be. While we are in one sense slaves of Christ, we are also His friends as we live in obedience to Him. He could say this to His disciples because He had told them everything God had revealed to Him.

Blessings through Jesus' love (John 15:16-17). Although it was common for followers to choose which teacher they wanted to learn from, Jesus reminded His disciples that in His case He had done the choosing.

Jesus always remains central, and our prayers should be presented to the Father in His name. Finally, we must remember His great command: we who are His children should love each other, even sacrificially.

—Keith E. Eggert.

QUESTIONS

1. Who was Jesus referring to when He spoke of the vine, the husbandman, and the branches?
2. What might it mean that God takes away unfruitful branches?
3. What does God do to give His children further opportunity for spiritual growth?
4. What is necessary if a Christian is going to produce spiritual fruit for the Lord?
5. What does it mean for God to take the unfruitful branches and cast them into the fire?
6. What is one rewarding result that comes from abiding in Christ?
7. What is a second rewarding result?
8. In what way did Jesus say that believers should love one another?
9. What is the highest standard of love that can be shown to anyone?
10. How can we be both a slave and a friend of our Lord?

—Keith E. Eggert.

PRACTICAL POINTS

1. Following Jesus is not an easy task, but through all the hardships, we can be certain that God's desire is to make us more fruitful (John 15:1-3).
2. The believer's fruitfulness is wholly dependent on his relationship with Christ (vss. 4-5).
3. Spiritual fruit is the mark of a true Christian (vss. 6-8).
4. Jesus' relationship to the Father is the model for our relationship to Christ (vss. 9-10).
5. The fruitful life is a joyful life (vs. 11).
6. True love is at the core of our relationship with God and with other Christians (vss. 12-17).

—Ralph Woodworth.

RESEARCH AND DISCUSSION

1. The stress on "the true vine" in John 15:1 suggests the possibility of a false vine. What might that false vine be?
2. In what ways does God purge, or prune, us to make us more fruitful (vs. 2)?
3. What is the "fruit" that Christ expects from every believer (John 15:2; cf. Rom. 1:13; 6:22; Gal. 5:22-23)?
4. What is the relationship between bearing fruit and being a disciple of Christ (John 15:8; cf. Matt. 3:8; Rom. 7:4; Col. 1:10)?
5. How is it possible for us to love one another as Christ loves us (John 15:12; cf. Rom. 12:9; I Thess. 3:12; I Pet. 1:22)?

—Ralph Woodworth.

Golden Text Illuminated

"I am the vine, ye are the branches: He that abideth in me, and I in him, the same bringeth forth much fruit: for without me ye can do nothing" (John 15:5).

Jesus and His disciples had just left the upper room and were on their way to the Garden of Gethsemane when our lesson text for this week begins. Perhaps they had passed by a vineyard on their way, and Jesus took it as an opportunity to begin teaching about Himself as the True Vine.

In claiming to be the vine, Jesus was rightfully claiming to be the fulfillment of all that God had intended His covenant people to be. He is the true seed of Abraham, in whom all the nations of the world have been blessed (cf. Gen. 12:3; 18:18; 22:18; 26:4; 28:14). Through Jesus Christ, salvation and the righteousness of God through faith has been spread throughout the world (cf. Rom. 3:21-22; Phil. 3:9).

But what exactly did Jesus mean when He spoke of "abiding?" The Lord provides additional clues in verses 7 and 10, adding that abiding in Him has to do with keeping His word and His commands. So a person who keeps Christ's word in his heart and obeys Him is abiding in Him.

To state the issue as simply as possible, we can say that abiding in Christ equates to remaining His disciples; that is, testifying by our words and actions that we belong to Him.

Without Christ we can do nothing of spiritual benefit. Pray for abiding faith and obedience in your life—abide in the True Vine!

—John Lody.

Scripture Lesson Text

JOHN 17:6 I have manifested thy name unto the men which thou gavest me out of the world: thine they were, and thou gavest them me; and they have kept thy word.

7 Now they have known that all things whatsoever thou hast given me are of thee.

8 For I have given unto them the words which thou gavest me; and they have received *them,* and have known surely that I came out from thee, and they have believed that thou didst send me.

9 I pray for them: I pray not for the world, but for them which thou hast given me; for they are thine.

10 And all mine are thine, and thine are mine; and I am glorified in them.

11 And now I am no more in the world, but these are in the world, and I come to thee. Holy Father, keep through thine own name those whom thou hast given me, that they may be one, as we *are.*

12 While I was with them in the world, I kept them in thy name: those that thou gavest me I have kept, and none of them is lost, but the son of perdition; that the scripture might be fulfilled.

13 And now come I to thee; and these things I speak in the world, that they might have my joy fulfilled in themselves.

14 I have given them thy word; and the world hath hated them, because they are not of the world, even as I am not of the world.

15 I pray not that thou shouldest take them out of the world, but that thou shouldest keep them from the evil.

16 They are not of the world, even as I am not of the world.

17 Sanctify them through thy truth: thy word is truth.

18 As thou hast sent me into the world, even so have I also sent them into the world.

19 And for their sakes I sanctify myself, that they also might be sanctified through the truth.

20 Neither pray I for these alone, but for them also which shall believe on me through their word;

21 That they all may be one; as thou, Father, *art* in me, and I in thee, that they also may be one in us: that the world may believe that thou hast sent me.

NOTES

Jesus Prays for Believers

Lesson Text: John 17:6-21

Related Scriptures: Luke 22:31-32; John 17:22-24; Hebrews 7:24-27

TIME: A.D. 30   PLACE: Jerusalem

GOLDEN TEXT—"[I pray] that they all may be one; as thou, Father, art in me, and I in thee, that they also may be one in us: that the world may believe that thou hast sent me" (John 17:21).

Lesson Exposition

PRAYER FOR GOD'S GLORY— John 17:6-8

Through keeping God's word (John 17:6). The lengthy prayer of Jesus recorded in John 17 took place on the night of His betrayal and shortly before His arrest in Gethsemane. He apparently prayed these words after leaving the upper room.

First, Jesus prayed that God would glorify Him so that through Him God would be glorified (John 17:1-6). His prayer then turned to His disciples. Jesus had manifested God's name to these men; that is, He fully revealed God's nature and character to them through His words and His works.

These men, whom the Father had given to Jesus from out of the world, had kept God's word. They had their failings, but the course of their lives was one of obedience to God.

Through knowing the truth (John 17:7-8). Jesus affirmed that at this point the disciples had come to understand that everything Jesus had been given was indeed given by the Father. Their obedience and understanding were means by which He would be glorified. Thus, these words establish the importance of the subsequent petitions of Jesus on the disciples' behalf.

PRAYER FOR THE DISCIPLES— John 17:9-19

To confirm their position (John 17:9-10). Jesus' disciples were the particular objects of His prayer here. They were the ones through whom Jesus would be glorified after His return to heaven. So certain was Jesus' glorification in them that He stated it as if it were already accomplished. It must have greatly encouraged the disciples as they heard this.

To give them unity (John 17:11-12). Jesus knew that He would soon leave His disciples behind. Therefore, He asked the Father to "keep" them and to preserve their unity. When He asked the Father to keep His disciples and said, "I kept them in thy name," He was probably referring to keeping them from evil, or the evil one.

Jesus prayed that the disciples would "be one" (vs. 11) just as He and the Father are one. This speaks not of some outward, organizational unity but of an inward, spiritual one.

To give them joy (John 17:13). Jesus looked forward to the joy He would soon experience in the Heavenly Father's presence. His desire was that the disciples know that joy as well.

To protect them (John 17:14-15). Because the disciples had been given God's word, or message, and had accepted it, thereby identifying with God and God's Son, they were not a part of the world. It was therefore certain that the world would hate them.

Jesus' prayer, therefore, was that God would protect them in the world, that He would "keep them from the evil" (vs. 15). "The evil" here refers to Satan, the evil one.

The disciples had God's message; what they needed now was His protection as they faced the temptations and attacks of Satan.

To sanctify them (John 17:16-17). Jesus' prayer was that God the Father would sanctify the disciples through His truth. He further identified the truth with God's Word. To sanctify means "to make holy" or "set apart."

Jesus was talking about the progressive setting apart of believers as they grow in holiness. This type of sanctification is accomplished by the Word (Eph. 5:25-26). The "word" in John 17:17 here refers to the truths Jesus had given them. These truths are now contained in the Bible.

To equip them (John 17:18-19). Jesus' words here again reinforce the need for the disciples' protection (vs. 15) and sanctification (vs. 17). Just as the Father had sent Jesus into the world, so Jesus had sent His disciples out. Both Jesus and the disciples were sent to take God's message of salvation to a hostile world.

Jesus said that it was for His followers' sakes that He sanctified Himself. The primary idea here seems to be that Jesus sanctified, or set Himself apart, for death.

PRAYER FOR FUTURE BELIEVERS—John 17:20-21

The focus of the Lord's prayer now turned to a wider group. It was through the apostles of Jesus—through their personal ministries and writings—that future believers would come to faith in Christ. It was for all these subsequent believers that He now prayed.

How wonderful it is to know that even as Jesus faced the cross, He prayed for us, and He prayed that we might be unified! His desire for us is that we be united as one in Him and in the Father. There is no closer unity than that which exists between God the Father and God the Son. This kind of unity is the pattern for our unity with God and with one another.

—Jarl K. Waggoner.

QUESTIONS

1. What was the setting of Jesus' prayer in John 17?
2. How had Jesus manifested God's name to His disciples (vs. 6)?
3. What did Jesus affirm about the disciples' spiritual understanding?
4. From what did Jesus ask the Father to keep His disciples?
5. What kind of unity did Jesus want for His disciples?
6. Why would the world hate the disciples after Jesus' departure?
7. What did Jesus pray in light of that?
8. What did Jesus mean when He asked the Father to sanctify the disciples (vs. 17)?
9. How is personal sanctification accomplished?
10. What did Jesus pray in regard to us?

—Jarl K. Waggoner.

PRACTICAL POINTS

1. Jesus' gracious love for us displays God and His glory to the world (John 17:6-10).
2. We should seek unity with one another that will in some sense reflect the unity within the Trinity (vs. 11).
3. We do not have to worry about an evil power being stronger than Jesus (vs. 12).
4. Knowledge of God's truth will sanctify us as we live in the world (vss. 13-19).
5. Jesus prayed for all His followers in the future to be unified, including you and me (vss. 20-21).

—Stuart Olley.

RESEARCH AND DISCUSSION

1. Who are the people God has given to Jesus (John 17:6-10, 20)? Was Jesus praying for believers today?
2. What can the members of our local church do to reflect something of the unity within the Trinity (John 17:11; cf. Eph. 4:1-6)?
3. How certain can we be that God will save us if we have faith in Him (John 17:12; cf. 10:27-30)?
4. What are some of the practices that help us in sanctification (17:13-19)? How can our progress in sanctification be a witness in the world (Col. 4:5-6)?
5. How does Jesus' prayer for you encourage you (John 17:20-21)?
6. What gifts does God equip us with that are part of His nature (John 17:22-26; cf. II Pet. 1:3-11)?

—Stuart Olley.

Golden Text Illuminated

"[I pray] that they all may be one; as thou, Father, art in me, and I in thee, that they also may be one in us: that the world may believe that thou hast sent me" (John 17:21).

"By this shall all men know that ye are my disciples, if ye have love one to another" (John 13:35). Our relationships with fellow believers are important to our Saviour. In His last recorded prayer with His disciples (nearly all of John 17), He prayed that His followers would be unified in love. The reason is listed twice: that the world would know that Jesus was sent from God.

A song from 1968 declares, "And they'll know we are Christians by our love" (Scholtes). Many like to conclude that the world will know that Jesus was sent from God because of our love for the lost. But according to Jesus, it is our love for each other that proves to the world that He is who He said He is.

So, if our world does not believe that Jesus was sent from God, we may be partly at fault. Many believe Christ was merely a good man or a good teacher. We know that is not enough. However, this passage shows us that what will convince people is not just ardent evangelism, careful argumentation, or even great compassion for the lost. Our love for one another as Christians will also be crucial.

A church of believers who are unified by Jesus' love could change the world! Sometimes it is easier to love the lost than it is to love our brothers and sisters in Christ, but we must make brotherly love a priority.

—Kimberly Rae.

PARAGRAPHS ON PLACES AND PEOPLE

TREASURY (OF THE TEMPLE)

As the book of Joshua makes clear, Israel needed a place where they could store their treasures dedicated to God (cf. 6:19, 24). David's instructions to Solomon for the temple included a treasury (I Chr. 28:12). Solomon's temple contained a place for storing the gold and silver that was dedicated to the Lord (I Kgs. 5:17). In the time of Jesus, the priests served as administrators of the treasures in the temple.

The exact location of the temple treasury has been disputed, but because women had access to giving offerings, it is thought to have been located by the Court of the Women, which was located in the outer court, past the Beautiful Gate. There were boxes, with openings shaped like inverted megaphones, that were positioned to receive the donations of the worshippers. Jesus saw the widow give her two mites there (Mark 12:41).

JESUS' TOMB

For centuries, emperors, kings, historians, archaeologists, and filmmakers have searched for the location of Jesus' temporary tomb. Most Bible scholars will caution that there is not enough proof of its exact location.

Two locations are the main contenders. The first contender is the Garden Tomb, also known as Gordon's Tomb, named after Charles Gordon, who discovered a tomb two-hundred-and-seventy-five yards outside Jerusalem, in a garden, near a rock formation that looked like a skull (supposedly Golgotha).

The second, and strongest, contender is the tomb in the Church of the Holy Sepulchre. In A.D. 325, Emperor Constantine sent a group to find the tomb. They followed local tradition that it was under a temple built by Emperor Hadrian in the second century. When they leveled the temple, they found a tomb underneath. They then built a shrine around it. Scholars verify that the tomb existed in the first century, but no one can say with certainty that Jesus rested there. Located in the Christian Quarter of the Old City, the site draws many visitors yearly.

ALL THAT ARE IN THE GRAVES

Jesus referred to the resurrection of the righteous and the unrighteous that would take place in the last day. Both will physically rise from their graves to stand before God, who will determine their eternal destinies. Christ's perfect work on the cross gives Him the authority to raise the dead to life. Those who have put their trust in Him will live for eternity in heaven.

ALL THOSE WHO CAME BEFORE ME

Jesus' statement in John 10:8 that all who came before Him were thieves and robbers must be taken within the context of His being the door of the sheepfold. He was not referring to Old Testament prophets, because none of them claimed to be the Messiah, and they all pointed to Him.

Jesus was talking about those who pretended to be the means by which all others could come to God. They claimed to be the mediators between man and God.

—Don Ruff.

Daily Bible Readings for Home Study and Worship

(Readings are for the week previous to the lesson topics.)

1. March 5. Jesus' Baptism

M — The Saviour and His Forerunner. Luke 1:67-80.
T — The Lamb of God. John 1:29-34.
W — Make Way for the Lord. Matt. 3:1-12.
T — Listen to My Son. Mark 9:2-8.
F — A Voice from Heaven. John 12:27-32.
S — Eyewitnesses to Christ's Majesty. II Pet. 1:16-21.
S — The Beloved Son. Mark 1:4-13.

2. March 12. Overcoming Temptation with the Word

M — God's Care in the Wilderness. Deut. 8:1-10.
T — Worship and Trust God. Ps. 95:1-11.
W — Resist the Devil. Jas. 4:7-12.
T — The Whole Armor of God. Eph. 6:10-20.
F — Stand Against Temptation. I Cor. 10:9-13.
S — Cast Your Cares upon Him. I Pet. 5:6-11.
S — Temptation in the Wilderness. Matt. 4:1-14a.

3. March 19. Doing the Father's Work

M — Made Whole by the Son. John 5:1-17.
T — In the Father's House. Luke 2:41-52.
W — Jesus Praises His Father. Luke 10:17-24.
T — Jesus Does What His Father Does. John 10:31-39.
F — Doing the Father's Will. John 8:25-30.
S — Obeying the Father. John 14:28-31.
S — The Son Honors the Father. John 5:19-29.

4. March 26. Submitting to the Father's Will

M — Placing Hope in God. Ps. 42:1-11.
T — Jesus' Hour Has Come. John 12:20-26.
W — Peace from Trusting Jesus. John 16:29-33.
T — Jesus' Work Complete. John 17:1-5.
F — The Will of Him Who Sent Me. John 6:37-40.
S — Cry Out to the Lord. Ps. 88:1-13.
S — Agony in the Garden. Matt. 26:36-50.

5. April 2. Crucified for Sinners

M — Jesus Sentenced to Die. Luke 23:13-31.
T — Christ's Death Foretold. Ps. 22:1-18.
W — Golgotha. John 19:16-24.
T — The Suffering Saviour. Isa. 53:3-12.
F — The Faith of the Thief. Luke 23:32-43.
S — It Is Finished. John 19:28-30.
S — Forsaken by God? Matt. 27:38-54.

6. April 9. Risen from the Dead! (Easter)

M — The Stone Rolled Away. Mark 16:1-11.
T — No Hope Without Resurrection. I Cor. 15:12-19.
W — God's Mighty Power. Eph. 1:15-23.
T — He Is Risen! Luke 24:1-12.
F — The Sign of Jonah. Matt. 12:38-42.
S — Not Abandoned to the Grave. Ps. 16:1-11.
S — An Empty Tomb. John 20:1-10, 19-20.

7. April 16. Proofs of the Resurrection

M — Many Infallible Proofs. Acts 1:1-4.
T — Christ Arose. I Cor. 15:3-8.
W — The Word of Life. I John 1:1-4.
T — Jesus with the Disciples. Mark 16:12-14.

F — The Road to Emmaus. Luke 24:13-35.
S — The Third Appearance. John 21:1-14.
S — Scripture Now Fulfilled. Luke 24:36-53.

8. April 23. The Bread of Life

M — The Feeding of the Five Thousand. John 6:1-13.
T — God Sends Manna. Ex. 16:4-18.
W — Complaints About Manna. Num. 11:4-10.
T — Judgment for Ungrateful Hearts. Ps. 78:17-31.
F — God's Mercy on Mankind. Isa. 55:1-7.
S — One with Christ. John 6:47-58.
S — The True Bread from Heaven. John 6:22-35.

9. April 30. The Light of the World

M — A Light to the Nations. Isa. 9:2-4.
T — The True Light. John 1:1-10.
W — Believers Shine Forth in the World. Phil. 2:12-16.
T — Life Through the Son. I John 5:5-13.
F — Out of the Darkness into the Light. John 3:16-21.
S — The Path of the Just. Prov. 4:14-22.
S — The Light of Life. John 8:12-20; 12:44-46.

10. May 7. The Good Shepherd

M — The Lord Is My Shepherd. Ps. 23:1-6.
T — The Lord's Flock. Ezek. 34:10-25.
W — Peter Commissioned to Shepherd. John 21:15-17.
T — Shepherd the Flock. I Pet. 5:1-4.
F — He Will Feed His Flock. Isa. 40:9-14.
S — Perfect in Every Good Work. Heb. 13:20-21.
S — The Door to Eternal Life. John 10:7-18.

11. May 14. The Resurrection and the Life

M — The Death of Lazarus. John 11:1-16.
T — Lazarus Raised to Life. John 11:28-45.
W — Awakening to Life or to Shame. Dan. 12:1-3.
T — The Resurrection of the Dead. I Cor. 15:20-26.
F — The Power of His Resurrection. Phil. 3:7-14.
S — The Resurrection of the Just and Unjust. Acts 24:10-21.
S — Those in Christ Will Never Die. John 11:17-27.

12. May 21. The True Vine

M — The Parable of the Vineyard. Isa. 5:1-7.
T — The Lord's Vineyard. Isa. 27:2-6.
W — Rooted in Christ. Col. 2:6-10.
T — A Fruitless Vine. Ezek. 15:1-8.
F — A Vine out of Egypt. Ps. 80:8-19.
S — My Servant the Branch. Zech. 3:6-10.
S — Abide in Me. John 15:1-17.

13. May 28. Jesus Prays for Believers

M — Our High Priest and Intercessor. Heb. 7:24-27.
T — Jesus Prays for our Oneness with God. John 17:22-26.
W — The Lord Prays for Peter's Faith. Luke 22:24-34.
T — Believe and Confess Jesus Is Lord. Rom. 10:5-17.
F — The Lord's Favor. Isa. 61:1-11.
S — Ask in Confidence. I John 3:19-24.
S — Prayer for Protection. John 17:6-21.